Endorsements

2nd Line West by Tom Herstad is a loving tribute to his mother, Margie, who spent her life selflessly in service to those she encountered in the path of life. Margie's light was truly exceptional, and she has managed to touch my heart, even though she's not here with us today. This book will truly leave you better than it found you and encourage you to live your life with courage and compassion for those around you.

—Christine Lee,
International Bestselling author of *My Hero*

"A book is a tool that can be used as a pointer for the reader to look within, but not every book does this. Tom's book, *2nd Line West*, does this and can be used to enhance one's life."

—Michael Cupo,
author of *"It's Monday Only in Your Mind"*

"How I wish I'd had the pleasure of meeting your mother in my lifetime. The overwhelming love, care, and share is how I live my life. The similarities between the anecdotes you share about your life and your mother's and my own are insane. A few examples, apart from the obvious, is my home is where all my children's friends come to feel peace, sleep, or eat and get advice with absolutely no judgment. Whatever I can give, I will try. My grandmother lost her leg to gangrene when my children were young, and my connection with my mother and hers to me were overwhelmingly similar to your mom's and yours. My daughter was visited by white butterflies at various times, as I was, shortly after my grandmother's death, and we felt her presence and heard her in my mother's home after her passing.

We also dance in our home and live by your mother's creed almost daily. I agree with everything she believed in and only hope to continue my own path in her footsteps. With this book, I no longer feel alone. I always felt like I was being soft or 'too good,' as people often tell me. I do the things I do because we are all put here by God for a purpose. And mine is much like your mother's, as my grandmother's before me, and my mother's, too. I cried through the whole reading of this book and felt such joy and calm.

Thank you above all, Tom. We were meant to have that conversation on my porch that day. Your mother led you to me because it was the right thing for me.

Even never having met her, she made her presence known to me; she's truly an angel and still touching lives even after she is gone from this Earth.

I will continue to be true to myself and live by your mother's philosophy. Her story solidifies my values and my heart. Thank you most of all for sharing her with the world. What a lovely gift you have given me, to us all."

—Laura Paletta

"The book *2nd Line West* is a story of a family and more specifically a mother's journey. This story reminds us of something we are born with; something that most everyone has forgotten along the way. As we are reminded, we remember how to enjoy closer relationships, love easier and better, experience a more fulfilling life."

—Reigan Gerald Franklin

2nd Line West, a book that touches all! I always have great respect for people like Tom Herstad, who acknowledges and pays tribute to his mother, giving the best example to all of us!

It's a beautiful way to say thank you to someone we love and admire whether it is a mother, a father, a friend, or someone with a golden heart like Margie's...an incredible lady, Mrs Margie Herstad!

—Maria Xenidou,
International Bestselling author of *Socrates and Soc*

"Tom Herstad's *2nd Line West* is a love letter to all mothers who have treated their family, friends, and all those in need with compassion and understanding.

Reading about Tom's mom Margie's life is akin to reading and vicariously experiencing a spiritual master's life—though a single, widowed mother of four children, she opened her home to the less fortunate so that troubled teens, homeless people, and a drug-addicted biker could experience what it's like to have a home and a family. In our troubled times, we need to acknowledge and pay tribute to the Margie Herstad's of the world—which is what Tom Herstad does so beautifully in his meticulously crafted work."

—Tom Schlesinger, motion picture writer-producer

2nd Line West is a powerful narrative written about a woman who cared and loved through the challenges and celebrations of her life. This book captivates readers with imagination and visual imagery that paints the backdrop of Tom's childhood. His mother is the modern-age hero we need in the 21st century.

—Roslyn Rice,
Bestselling author of *Power of One*

"I read every single word of this book, *2nd Line West*. I could not put it down. It is obvious to me that your mother is working through you. I also believe she has guided me to this book. I truly understand your mom's gift and messages, her understanding of God, our life journey, her willingness to share her light, her gifts with those who crossed her path, and how her actions changed people for the better. The author's ability to communicate the goodness of God through the energy and messages that flowed through his mom's story is incredible. These messages are both bricks and butterflies, hitting hard and gently simultaneously. His writing so beautifully shared his mother's spirit!"

—Paula Williams

2nd Line West is one of those stories that you instantly know were written from the heart. Tom Herstad's powerful storytelling truly captures the essence of an exceptional woman who lived her life impacting every soul she came across, forever moving them with her kindness and compassion. This is an exceptional read, and I am confident that the life of Margie will encourage readers to branch out of their comfort zones and offer their hearts to all those in need.

—Judy O'Beirn,
President & CEO of Hasmark Publishing International

"Tom Herstad has done a lovely job of sharing with us the amazing story of his mother, Margie, and his family in *2nd Line West*. I highly recommend this book for any individual or family wishing deeper and more loving connections with each other."

—Paul Saltzman,
Emmy Award-winning Movie and Television Director/Producer

To: _____

To: _____

To: _____

2nd Line West

"Love, Care and Share"

by

TOM HERSTAD

Hasmark PUBLISHING INTERNATIONAL

Hasmark
PUBLISHING
INTERNATIONAL

Table of Contents

Acknowledgments

This book is a memoir. I thank members of my family, friends, and contacts for allowing me to share their contributions to this book on my mother's life and her impact on others.

The stories I have written are purely my memories of the events, from my own perspective. Some events have been compressed, and some dialogue has been recreated, including others' tributes and the interviews, which were compiled by my sister, Julie.

Far from intending or hinting at any criticism of anyone, this book is a loving homage to Margie.

Please see full acknowledgments at the end of the book.

Special Acknowledgment

All the interviews herein were transcribed to print by Julie. All the collaborative efforts of family and friends that were included in this book have enabled me to share the amazing story of Margie, a loving mother, grandmother, sister, aunt, and a wonderful friend to oh, so many.

Connect with Tom Herstad: www.TomHerstadOfficial.com

Dedication

This book is dedicated to you, the reader. If not for you, Margie's message would go unnoticed.

"The effect you have on others is the most valuable currency there is."

—Jim Carrey

"To all who seek new patterns of peace and walk the path with heart."

—Diane Dreher,
from *The Tao of Inner Peace*

Preface

While preparing to write this book, I scheduled a trip to Cuba at a remote resort on the peninsula of Cayo Coco to centre myself. I wanted to sit in a lawn chair, stare at the stars, gaze at the ocean, read the *Autobiography of a Yogi*, eat fresh lobster, and ride a scooter around the peninsula at daybreak. For clarity, I needed to walk along the shore to find my inner spiritual strength to make some decisions before embarking on this impending book completion commitment. I also realized that I had to make a decision to myself to finish something I did not know how to do. How do I find an editor? How can I get a book published? How do I do any of this?

My youngest sister, Julie, came along; we initiated this work four years ago after my mother's passing. It was clearly time to blow more wind into the sail of this labour of love. My fun-loving sister would also bring depth of conversation.

Whether we view serendipitous occurrences in our lives as mere coincidences, I learned "God-incidence" (as my mother had often called it) was at work right here on my way to Cayo Coco.

When I took my aisle seat, I was glad to be seated next to a quiet couple. I could simply rest and read. For the first hour, that was what I did. Then I looked up and we connected, discussing the woman's interior design business, among her other creative work, and my lighting business based in Toronto. I shared my love of reading spiritual books and the importance of family and love. When I mentioned my impending writing project, I realized that I had been randomly seated beside a published author who was an editor and an independent publisher. What are the odds of that? For the rest of our flight, I got to know Tanya Freedman and her husband, Austin, who weighed in with his life coaching and counselling experience. It was one of those, "Oh, that was quick, we're landing!" flights. Time was nowhere in the exciting, engaging experience.

One week later in the Cuba airport, I sat with my new green leaf coconut hat awaiting my flight. Here was Tanya walking towards me. This time we exchanged business cards and promised to keep in touch. On the plane taking my seat, I realized that I was seated next to her again. On both flights! What are the odds of this?

Then, as we kept sharing our thoughts, when and where each of us was born, we discovered that Tanya and my mother shared the same birthday, May 14th. Was this a God-incidence at work?

I told Tanya why I felt compelled to write this book, sharing stories. Despite her various projects, she agreed to receive the writing I had completed and would give me her opinion on whether this might be a book for our family, or if there was a bigger purpose. I assured her she need not worry about offending me with any of her personal and professional responses.

I emailed Tanya my initial sixty-eight-page draft, and waited. When she called me two weeks later, she said, "I'm all in with you on this book, Tom. It's uplifting and a great gift to us all. Your mother was a unique woman. We're going to do something wonderful together and share and celebrate her life with the world."

Tanya's statement initiated my decision to take four months off from my lighting business to focus on this book's completion and publish the first Edition.

Introduction

The first time I saw the house on the country road 2nd Line West, it was the summer of 1971. I was seven years old. This was the place where many lives were changed forever, including my own.

Our father, a busy real estate broker, simply fell in love when he first saw this particular country home during a showing to his clients. Oh no, he could not sell this special place to anyone else. Mom and Dad bought this house as an investment property. They knew our family would call this beautiful place home one day. It was a ranch bungalow, sprawling from left to right, with light-coloured brick and a black roof, sitting in the middle of two acres of land. There was a separate black wood tool shed on the right side of the property, an in-ground pool with diving board at the back left corner, and a pool house with change rooms. An eighty-foot drive-way with lush hedges running down each side brought you into the property. The front yard had two large cedar trees, a white birch tree, and a decorative wood structure that covered the well water shaft; it looked like a tiny white house.

As my father drove the forty-five minutes north from our sub-urban home near Toronto to 2nd Line West, one mile from the little village of Meadowvale, he explained to me the benefits of living in the country. I sat in the front seat of his new silver Monte Carlo, looking up at him, my eyes wide, hanging on to his every word. The car windows were all the way down as the wind rushed in. I noticed different smells in the air the further we got away from the city. Dad had a special nickname for me. "Zeek, nature is a place that helps us think, get to know ourselves, have a more open mind. Out here, son, where children don't have a local mall to hang out, families have closer relationships with one another."

As we pulled into the driveway, he parked on the paved extension behind the house and got out of the car. He said, "Come on with me." He walked to the back of the property and ducked through the middle of the wooden fence railing. Of course, I followed him into a golden hay field that surrounded the house. The field took my breath away as we stood amongst what looked like millions of gold feathers, waist high for Dad and chest high for me. In the gentle wind, gold dust swirled around us, sparkling, as it deflected the sunlight. This was the pollen dust released from the hay, which we disturbed as we made our way through. I followed in his footsteps, which made a path, an easier walk for me.

We continued in silence for ten minutes or so over the rolling fields, then climbed up to the top of a knoll. We stopped to survey the Credit River far off in the distance. We could now see down into the valley. Next to the river were train tracks and a wooden trestle bridge over the water.

Dad paused, looking across and down at all this beauty. It was late in the afternoon. The sun was about to set, sending warm-coloured light that blanketed the scenery. To me, everything was brilliant. The distant green fields looked greener, the Credit River, a darker blue hue, the gold hay field, more golden as it swayed and swirled in the wind around us. I looked up at Dad and saw him smile to himself. Professional photographers call this time of day the magic hour for a reason. We continued to gaze over the landscape, and then he turned to me. "Zeek, you might not be able to see what I'm looking at right now, but there'll be a day when you'll see everything I'm seeing. The beauty of this place will overwhelm and surprise you." I simply nodded and took his hand.

Our family did move into this country home on 2nd Line West two years later. We spent many years here together, but only two as an entire family. My father's death occurred in the winter of 1975. It took years for our family to recover from losing him, especially our mother, who lost the love of her life. Now Margie, at thirty-eight, with a grade-six education, was a widow with four children. Along with her shock and grieving, she had to reinvent herself.

Everything had to change. Everything.

As a wonderful mother, full of fun, focus, and determination that surrounded her caring for the four of us, Margie continued her approach to life. She continued to offer our spare bedroom to many who came across her path. That room was rarely empty. But it was how and why she was able to do this that is her amazing story, and my honour to tell. Margie had a naturally caring disposition that allowed her to always notice someone who needed help, a place to land, a place to regroup after life offered them up depression, sad-ness, or an unexpected "curve ball." The home on 2nd Line West was a place where many were given their second chance, and some even a third chance, not just us kids.

Fast forward to the late summer of 2011. We lost her at the early age of seventy-three. Our mother's memorial service had just taken place. My youngest sister, Julie, and I were driving through the countryside not far from our old home on 2nd Line West; we left that house in 1983. As we drove by the property, I lingered a bit as we remembered those who did take our spare bedroom. This was a home Mom brought people to, offering them respite and safety. When Julie and I finished remembering the many who stayed with us in the late 1970s forward, we were shocked that the list totalled eighteen people. "Let's go find them, Julie," I said, sitting in the car, thinking of our beloved Mom. "Let's interview them on how their time in our home and how their relationship with our mother helped them in their life journey."

We did. It took us three years. Through word of mouth and social media, we were able to find everyone and completed all interviews. Some also wrote us letters. I've always had a deep respect for my mother, honouring her throughout my life. Yet conducting these interviews took my admiration, respect, and awe to a whole new level. My mother's story and these people's stories had to be told and shared with the world, this I knew.

After the interviews were completed, I began to write, often waking up in the middle of the night. I couldn't go back to sleep until a particular story was purged from my mind. Late one night, I sat at my desk wondering why Mom actually brought these people into our home. What was it about my mother that allowed her to do this so naturally? Grown up, in business, I sat in my home, an old farmhouse, in the upper loft. I gazed around the room. All walls were filled with pink paper, yes, Mom's favourite colour. I printed and pinned the stories and interviews up on all four walls. While this was always a quiet and serene place for my writing, this night at 3 am the silence was deafening. All of these stories represented our mother's natural response to another person in need. An individual who required some attention, care, and respect. As I sat, so still with hands resting on my laptop, a question occurred to me. Perhaps the desire to connect and help one another is something we are born with and something most everyone has forgotten.

I followed this thought further. I thought about a group of young children in a playground; if one falls down, another child immediately will respond by helping them up. I thought about a child in a daycare, moving a play table and chairs from the corner of the room to the middle. Other children automatically pitch in to move the pieces. I then remembered my mother's favourite life motto, "To love another is a gift that we give to ourself."

I am about to take you on a journey into a life story. The tragedy, struggle, rising, and continuing to move forward, onward. You will witness a lady's life, peek into a family's story, and then hear the stories from those our mother helped, her impact on those around her. She used her wisdom and strength to influence and facilitate positive transformations of many lives, all the while reinventing herself. I also share some parts of my own story and my thoughts with you.

Oh, I did see what my father said I would. It occurred two years after his death. I was fourteen, on a ten-speed bicycle pedalling up the big hill just south of our home on 2nd Line West; the Davidson horse farm was at the top of that hill. In autumn, vibrant colours in the trees bordered the country road. Standing on the bike pedals, with legs burning, I continued pumping my feet. My head facing downward, sweat dripping. As I pedalled in the shade of this hill, I felt the lowering air temperature on this beautiful late fall afternoon. It took all I had to pedal up that second tier of the steep incline. When I got to the summit, stopping, I looked up. The sun was setting directly in front of me over 2nd Line West. It was a brilliant orange. I felt its warmth on my face. A flock of about a hundred black birds flew towards me, passing ten feet above, all in formation. I heard the sound of their collective wings as they passed, a new sound I'd never heard before and have never heard since. I got off and stood on that paved, isolated country road, and said to myself, "Oh, my God! This is what he saw."

This was 2nd Line West.

Margie's Principles

Mary Margaret Herstad was born May 14th, 1938, in Dominion, Cape Breton Island, Nova Scotia. She impacted us with her own definition of Love, Care, and Share. Although she never spoke each of these definitions verbally, her actions confirmed them:

LOVE: You can never tell me anything about yourself or your behaviour that will change my opinion of you. You will know that I love you by the way I listen to you, by the way I look at you, by the way I talk to you, and I will tell you that I love you.

CARE: I will give you my time. I will listen to you. I will hear you. I will see you. Whatever you may need, I will try to provide, even if it seems beyond my means.

SHARE: I will tell you intimate stories about my life. I will put my pride aside. I will expose the wonderful, the bad, and the ugly. I will share my stories as a gift; we are more alike than different. My intent is to allow you to know that it's always going to be all right.

Chapter 1

Her Journey's Start

Margie, age 4, East Coast

Margie's Childhood

In 1943, when Margie was five years old, her father left the small Dominion of Cape Breton to find work out west. He sent his money home to care for the family. Margie had an older brother and two sisters. Their troubled mother and their absent father never reunited. At one time her mother's alcoholism got so bad that her family tried to commit her to a psychiatric hospital.

During much of this time, Margie had to stay with her Aunt Mayme, who taught her how to cook and care for a home.

Margie attended Catholic school where she suffered cruelty at the hands of the nuns who ran it. She left after grade six and was glad to be out of that environment. Times were tough in the East Coast as she and her siblings moved to Niagara Falls, Ontario, separately, when places became available for them. Eleven-year-old Margie arrived at Niagara Falls and got a job in a canning factory. She also helped at the local hospital. She was quick to offer a helping hand wherever she went. From a young age, she was able to see opportunities to make a difference.

Margie was a beautiful, bright, spirited girl with blonde, wavy hair and warm blue eyes. While boys wished she would look their way, she was only interested in her work. She grew up quickly and seemed mature for her every age.

Elaine Bell, Dad's cousin, described Mom: "I met Margie when I was fourteen, in 1956, at a Niagara-on-the-Lake beach, at the foot of King Street. Margie was an absolutely beautiful blue-eyed blonde, with a gorgeous figure. She wore a shirred white bathing suit. A few years later, I purchased a similar white bathing suit, hoping I looked half as good! Although Margie wasn't much older than me, I looked up to her as a worldly character, coming from out east and all. She was always kind to me, helping me in so many ways. I'll never forget her.

Mom loved to dance at the local dance hall, and this is where she eventually met her husband-to-be, Gerald Thomas Herstad, known as Gerry.

When Gerry first saw seventeen-year-old Margie at a dance, he said to his buddy, "That's the girl I'm going to marry." They became close friends.

Teenage Pregnancy

When Margie was seventeen, she had become pregnant by another man. Abortion was not an option for her or her Catholic family.

Gerry was a true friend, whom she completely trusted to help her with a life-changing decision. He supported her through the pregnancy and picked her up from the hospital after she gave birth to a baby girl.

Margie had just given the baby up for adoption, and broke down in the car, crying uncontrollably.

"Let's go back and get her?" Gerry voiced.

"We can't do that, she's meant for another!"

"Marry me and we can keep her," Gerry expressed. "I love you, Margie, always will."

"But I don't love you," Margie replied.

"I love you enough for both of us," he retorted.

At this moment in the car, Margie's tears fell down her beautiful pale face. Although it broke her heart to let go, she made the decision to allow the baby girl to be adopted by an infertile couple who had prayed for a baby for many years. They named the beautiful baby, Lee. Lee grew up as an only child and was treated like a princess.

Mom believed that we choose our parents at another level before conception. We choose them for the lessons we will learn with them.

Mom told each of us in our teens about Lee. I remember it well. Her face betrayed her vulnerability and fear, obviously wondering if it would change the way I felt and thought about her. I was able to say, "I can see how hard this was for you to tell me. I love you, Mom."

She burst into tears of pain, relief, and happiness. And she put her arms around me. When Mom was in her fifties, she decided to look for her daughter. At the same time Mom put in the request with the registering office, the adopted child put in her request. This process could take many years and sometimes never occurred—if both parties had not requested the reunion.

The process took three months. When Lee and Mom met, it became an exquisite time, and their relationship lasted for the rest of Mom's life.

Christmas used to be hard for Mom. It had represented the birth of the child she did not know. Lee was born on December 23rd. After their reunion, Christmas was enjoyed without grief.

Lee and I became closer during my preparation, for writing this book.

Lee was a gift Mom gave to another. I could hear Mom say, "We can be a conduit for others' wishes." Lee's full interview is included in later pages.

Love and Marriage

Mary Margaret initially resisted Gerry's attempts to take their relationship beyond friendship.

But he prevailed.

Ultimately, Margie would love Gerry completely, full force, full out, making him feel like he had never felt before. She always understood him more than he understood himself.

Margie was brought up Catholic while Gerry's family had no affiliations to any religion. When Margie was eighteen and Gerry was twenty-one, they met with the priest at her Catholic Church to discuss their impending marriage.

"I will perform the marriage ceremony here, but," the priest emphasized in his strong Irish accent, "only once you sign this agreement; it stipulates that your children will be brought up Catholic. They will attend church regularly."

Gerry stared at the priest and then looked at his fiancée. After a long moment he calmly said, "I'm sorry but I cannot sign an agreement which I will not honour."

"You're one of the most honest men I've ever met," the priest said, "But my hands are tied. I cannot marry you in this church without that signature."

Although Margie was disappointed, she agreed to marry Gerry and they chose another venue.

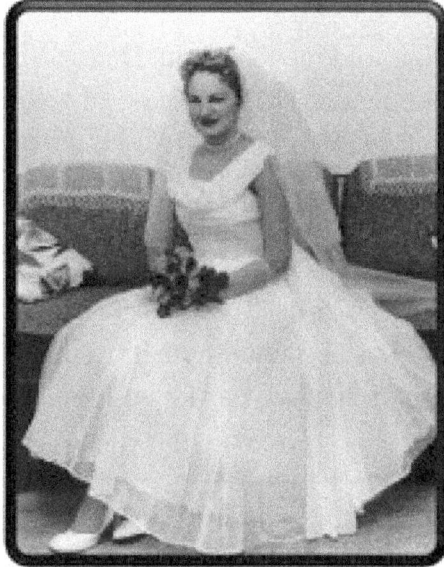

Margie, 18 years old

Margie and Gerry were married in Niagara-on-the-Lake at the United Church. The reception was at his parents' home on the gloriously sunny day of June 30, 1956. They took their wedding photos at the General Brock Monument. The food was laid out on a large table in the front yard and the festivities began. It was a small gathering.

Because their marriage ceremony did not take place in a Catholic Church, only her older sister Annabelle attended the wedding. That bittersweet day carried many conflicting emotions and memories.

Margie's growing love for her Gerry and their future together far outweighed the disappointment of not having all her family with her on that day. Gerry's Uncle Paul proudly walked her down the aisle.

The Love of Her Life

My parents' relationship was a tender love affair with a mix of fantastic, good, bad, and even some ugly. But they were always there for each other.

Years ago, Mom told me this about Dad, "When he walked into a room, women would notice him. The men would, too. The atmosphere in the room would change, and he did this without effort. You definitely wanted to know him."

The Journey Begins

Early on in my parents' marriage, Dad went into real estate after taking advice from a savvy businessman whom he respected. Dad was not shy when it came to approaching anyone for business or personal advice.

First home in the big city

After he earned his real estate licence, they moved to Toronto in 1956. Mom told me, "Tom, these first few years held some of the fondest memories we shared together."

They moved into their first home, putting everything they had into the down payment. Mom said, smiling, "We were just starting out in this big city together with pennies in our pockets. We didn't have dishes yet. On that first night in our new digs when we finished moving in, we found a can of beans in the cupboard. The previous owners must have left it. Exhausted, we both sat on the kitchen floor and Dad opened the can with a knife as we had no can opener," she said.

"I heated it on the stove and picked it up with our new washcloth so I wouldn't burn my fingers. I fished out a spoon from my purse and we handed the can of beans back and forth to each other. Eating and laughing at our predicament, it was a joyous new start together. One of the most wonderful meals I've ever had."

They would start a family quickly. First came Cyndy, and three years later, Valerie. When Mom gave birth to my middle sister, Valerie, she experienced complications in the operating room. She was hemorrhaging and the doctors were having trouble stopping the bleeding. Later, when I was in my teens, Mom told me how she felt herself floating above her body up to the corner of the room, overwhelmed with amazing contentment.

Why, she had never experienced this before! She recalled wondering, "Why are they working on me? I want to go; I'm fine."

Then remembering her daughter Cyndy at home, Mom thought, "'Who's going to take care of her and this new baby?' The next thing I remembered was the nurse calling my name." I came to, was staring up at the ceiling. I turned my head and locked eyes with the nurse.

They Are a Team

Dad became successful quickly at the real estate agency. He loved what he did and was a quick study, receiving sales awards as evidence. When upper management noticed him, he began to rub elbows with key players in the company. During an office get-together when wives were included, Mom overheard one of Dad's associates bragging about how he had sold an elderly lady a house with no plumbing. Mom witnessed Dad laughing with his colleagues during this story.

On the way home when he asked her why she was so silent, she expressed her concern for not only the associate's story, but also her husband's response to it. "I cannot even look at you right now," she said. From that day on, Dad made sure to stay on the path of integrity in his career.

At the end of that year, among other sales, Dad sold a house to a new immigrant couple who had two children. It was Christmas Eve and after making their down payment, the couple had no money left to celebrate Christmas. At their new home, Dad told them through the interpreter that he would be back in one hour.

He came home and shared the couple's situation with Mom. She instantly agreed that Dad should take our tree and presents to the new family to enjoy as their welcome gift to Canada. So, Christmas in our household with my two sisters, aged four and two, was delayed until Boxing Day. I was learning, through my parents' choices and deeds, that the effect of positive influences on others is our most valuable currency.

I recall talking with my mother about their early years together from her nursing home bed. She expressed how, when our father was about to make a decision in his career that involved others he worked with, he would invite them home for dinner. This gave her a chance to meet them and offer Dad her opinion, which helped him make his decision. She was helping him forge his career. They were a team!

There You Are

I was born in 1963, the one and only son. Julie was born in 1969. The Herstad family was complete.

My parents hosted many parties for their friends, and I remember how they looked at each other through the crowd as if there was no one else in the room. It also seemed to me that their friends, as a couple, were better when in the company of our parents. The party was always full of joy and celebration, everyone would dance.

As we grew up, our childhood friends loved stopping off at our house. Mom and Dad talked and listened to our friends and our home was a busy, happy place. Often, I would come home and see one of my friends leaving.

"What's up?"

"I dropped in to see your Mom. I'll call you later," my friend would say.

Sundays

For us four kids, Sunday after breakfast was music morning at our home. Our house was one of the oldest homes in the area on the perimeter of a high-income housing development called Westport. We settled in the living room on the lower extension of our home, which stretched out onto the apple orchard.

We could see it through the huge windowpanes on three sides of the large room with the huge central fireplace. We often heard birds hit the window as they thought they could fly through.

Mom and Dad played music on the hi-fi for us as we all sat on the couch. Kneeling in front of the hi-fi, sliding the front cabinet door to the left, as if he were opening a special box, Dad would then sell the song to us. He would engage us in a shared stare, then express, "Have I got a treat for you this morning." Then he would pause and say. "Are you ready?" After our enthusiastic, "Yes," there was another pause. "Are you sure?" Then he put on "Over the Rainbow" by Judy Garland or a piece by Frank Sinatra, Elvis Presley, Joan Baez, Roy Orbison, Harry Belafonte, Johnny Cash, Ray Price, Vicki Carr, Herb Albert, or Ray Charles.

My eldest sister, Cyndy, added Cat Stevens to the mix in her early teens. Our parents taught us that music was a magical, wonderful experience that helped us understand ourselves and other people. We learned that all types and styles of music evoked imagination and emotion.

We would all dance. As I write this, I wish all children would enjoy this type of morning with their parents and siblings.

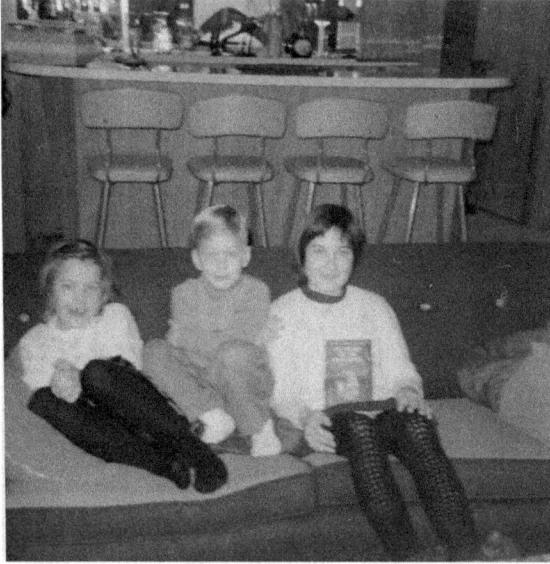

What will Dad play next?

Some mornings Dad would teach me to fight. He bought us two sets of boxing gloves. I put on my gloves and he put on only one glove. He got on his knees and held his glove out in front of him. "Keep your gloves up!"

Yet he always found a way through my defence and popped me on the forehead. He bobbed, weaved, and played, so I could not get him, laughing his smart-ass laugh.

"Come on, Tom, let's see what you got."

One morning he popped me pretty good a couple times. But during this fight, my sister said something to him. When he turned his head in distraction, I had my chance and cold-cocked him as hard as I could. He was so surprised that he hit me hard. When I started crying, he told me, "Don't ever sucker punch someone!" He taught me never to go looking for trouble, but you also never let anyone push you around.

Sunday dinners at our home were mandatory because Dad was in residential real estate, and frequently he was out during the week, so weekday dinners together were uncommon. On Sundays our parents taught us to say grace:

> "Thank you for the food we're about to receive and may we always be aware of the needs of others."

They made sure we sat properly, with elbows off the table, and at the end of dinner we asked to be excused from the table. We ate what was served, without complaint, and were expected to finish our plate.

Often on a Sunday, Dad loved to take me for a ride on his BSA 650 motorcycle. What a beautiful mechanical work of art, black with a red circle and starburst around it on the gas tank! It had a full fairing windshield. We put on our helmets and jackets, hugged and kissed Mom, who said to us, "Now boys, be careful, and watch out for the other guys, and watch out for all the other vehicles!" she'd add. "I want you home, safe!"

In the garage, Dad positioned the bike facing out, and after putting his gloves on, he turned it over with the kick-start. But it would not start. He adjusted the choke while continuously hammering the kick-start, over and over. After forty tries he removed his helmet. He continued for another dozen more tries; the jacket came off. With perspiration on his forehead, he finger-combed his hair out of his eyes.

I stood, quiet as a church mouse and ready for my cue...if and when it started. My coat was done up to the top button, my pants tucked into my socks, and my helmet securely fastened. I stood near Dad and the bike, still as a statue, sending positive energy and loaded with expectation. When would it start?

Well, sixty tries later, Dad sternly told me to get in the house and wait. Seeing his young son full of anticipation made him feel worse with every failed attempt.

Rushing back into the house, I leaned up against the glass window with my helmet. "He'll get her going, don't worry," Mom said, and smiled.

I looked out to see Dad pushing the bike down the driveway, wearing his helmet and blue and white motorcycle jacket, gloves on. He left my sight line and headed towards the road.

Suddenly, I heard the thundering engine and Dad shouting, "Come on, Tom, LET'S GO!"

I ran out of the house through the cloud of smoking exhaust and jumped up towards Dad, who helped me into position in front of him where the gas tank met the seat. I grabbed the bars on the fairing windshield and off we went!

LET'S GO!

One spring afternoon we stopped at Belfountain, a small town north of Toronto. Dad wanted coffee and I wanted ice cream. At that moment, fifty or sixty motor-bikes roared past us! Dad saw my mouth drop, my excited reaction to the mass of bikers and their leather jackets with the big crests on their backs. After they passed, it became quiet again.

"Tom," he said, "while you're looking at them, please know that is not what riding a motorcycle is about. It's about the wind, the road, the hills, and the dales. It's about what you see in the different landscapes and the smell in the air as you ride through a river valley. Those guys just need each other to feel strong and important."

I love writing this, feeling his presence, his complete commitment to get all his parenting in whenever he could.

Chapter 2

Growing Pains

Mom's definition of integrity: Do the right thing always, especially when no one's watching. You'll know the right thing to do: Simply check in and listen to your inner voice.

Is Margie There?

It was the spring of 1967 when we moved into a new neighbourhood. I was four. That's when Mom met Auntie Helen. We lived three houses away from each other on the same street. Before our move, my bike had been stolen. I guess I figured that if someone stole mine, it was okay for me to grab Auntie Helen's son's bike that first morning in the neighbourhood.

I jumped on it and started riding away. Auntie Helen came running after me as I rode back home. She yelled, "Come back here, you little bastard!"

When I got to our yard, Mom's head popped up from behind the hedges. "Who do you think you're calling a little bastard?"

Mom had me return the bike to their house and apologize to her son, David. This was the beginning of very special friendships. David and I became close friends, and Auntie Helen and Mom also became close.

Auntie Helen had many issues and was always on prescribed medication for depression and anxiety. She was a brilliant writer. She would call the house to speak with Mom, sometimes five times a day. When we answered the phone to her familiar and very distinct voice asking, "Is Margie there?" we would at times hold our hand over the phone and say that it was, *again*, Auntie Helen calling for Mom.

Mom would say, "Never you mind. Give me the phone," with a look, covering the mouthpiece, she would say, "You should be ashamed of yourself." Mom was teaching us that a friend in need is never a burden.

She took Auntie Helen's every call, any time. Auntie Helen dedicated a song to her: Anne

Murray's "You Needed Me."

I remember sharing this story with a friend of mine years later and he told me something profound: "I don't know of any other relationship in my forty-five years that demonstrated the same kind of faithful loyalty and support to another who was not a blood relative, who began just as a neighbour, as 'the nasty lady next door.' Your mother softened her. Margie knew she wasn't doing it just for Helen. No. She had Helen's daughters, son, and husband, Bob, in her mind and heart each and every time she took those calls."

We Shake Hands Now

I think I was five, going into my parents' room to say good night. We had always kissed and hugged Mom and Dad before bed. It was our family ritual.

On this particular evening after kissing and hugging Mom, I went around the other side of their bed about to put my arms around Dad. He extended his right hand to me. "You're too old for kissing and hugging. We'll shake hands now."

Why did he do that? Was he preparing me for manhood in his definition of it? I remember my deep sadness as I returned to my bed. I could no longer express my love and affection for him, while watching my sisters continue kissing and hugging Dad.

Thinking back on it, and understanding it from an adult per-spective, I believe this was the foundation of my suppressing many of my feelings for Dad. And, as a result, learning to curb feelings for others in my life.

Our parents taught us how to be and how not to be. But this, to me, was the latter. With my own son, I have always kissed and hugged him hello and goodbye. I want him to know I am open to his love and affection, always. Becoming the man he will be has nothing to do with pretending he cannot feel and experience love without it jeopardizing him as a man. I believe it will actually define him as a better man.

Mom must have talked about this to Dad. Later, in my childhood, I remember being able to hug him hello and goodbye. He had a light, musky smell with a hint of fresh aftershave I remember to this day.

Growing Wings

Mom walked me to kindergarten on my first day. The school was right behind our house. As we got to the half-way point in the schoolyard, I looked at her. "Mom, now I have to go from here on my own."

I remember her watching me go the rest of the way. Before I turned the corner out of view, I looked back. We shared a long, lov-ing look with each other—without a wave.

A Lesson

When I was six, Mom took my little sister, Julie, and me to Kmart. While putting candies in my pocket, to divert Mom's attention, I said that Julie was stealing.

Mom caught me: "Come here and take your hand out of your pocket!"

She marched me directly to the store manager: "Tell him that you stole from his store, Tom."

I did. The manager looked at me sternly. "I don't want you in here for one month. If you ever steal from the store again, you won't be allowed to come in here ever again. Is that understood?" My head lowered, I nodded.

Dad Changed in Front of Me

As I got older, I started seeing my parents' relationship in a different way. I saw its cracks and the human aspects I had not been aware of before. Cyndy was twelve years old, Valerie was nine, and I was six.

We all awoke in the middle of the night to hear Mom and Dad arguing. The commotion forced us out of bed, and we ran downstairs, following the raised voices out the front door into the driveway. Side by side, we three siblings stood on the gravel in our pyjamas, watching Mom take the keys from Dad. He wanted to drive after drinking. He had the car door open when she grabbed for the keys and they fell to the ground. They both dove for the keys, but Mom got them. Dad fell on top of her.

In shock, the adrenaline pumped through me. I ran across the gravel and jumped on my father's back. Sharp-edged rocks cut into my feet but it did not matter. Dad reached back to grab me and threw me to the ground.

In those seconds as he stared down at me, my father changed in front of me, from a sweating, wild-eyed demon to a desperate man. Hot liquid ran down the front of my pyjamas, as I lay on the driveway frozen to the spot.

Dad backed off, but continued to stare me down, and I trembled, scared to my core. Then he backed away even further.

In pain, I gingerly got up. My bare feet were raw from the jagged gravel. I turned to see my sisters standing behind me. They were paralyzed by what they had witnessed. Slowly the three of us walked silently back into the house.

Inside, we hugged each other, and I ran to the bathroom to clean myself up. Putting on fresh pyjamas, I got back, in bed to hide.

I never felt the same about Dad. Our whole family seemed to change, all of us now cautious around Dad.

After this night, although it did not happen often, whenever my parents got into an argument, Mom quickly came into my room. She knew Dad would not come here looking for her.

I realized that I had some power in our household. But, hearing my mother come into my room and lie down beside me, I pretended I was asleep so she would not wonder what I thought.

It was around this time that whenever my parents had a difference of opinion on any topic, I automatically sided with my Mom to push Dad away, to hurt him. Looking back, I wish I had not reacted to him in this manner. But I was six and my instinct took over. Clearly, it was not a conscious decision, but tragic all the same. But Dad certainly had a grateful side, which we did not see often.

He knew my mother believed in him more deeply than he believed in himself. She was the beacon for whom he could be, despite his insecurities.

It warms me recalling a certain day I was home sick from school in grade two or three. I witnessed Dad call home many times that day. I answered the phone all three times before handing it to Mom. When I asked her why he called that often she said, "Your father sometimes needs to hear my voice to get through a difficult day."

As we were growing up, whenever Dad was not home, Mom told us that he went fishing. This would happen after they had a long argument. Dad would go to a friend or family member's house to cool off. I even heard him express, "I won't be home tonight."

Protecting him and us, Mom knew children defined themselves through their parents to varying degrees, and she wanted to help us, his children, to believe in him as being good. This was a time when less was more, and Mom knew it.

Dad's Poem to Mom

I remember finding this poem in a card years later. It was a poem Dad wrote for Mom while he was in hospital.

> *Thank you*
>
> *For letting them think I was the mover,*
>
> *The shaker, The guy,*
>
> *When we both know It was you*
>
> *And not I.*

The Herstad Fun

My Mom and Dad also had lots of great fun times together. Whether they camped on their own, or we were all together, Dad loved surprising his wife. It was also not uncommon for him to frighten Mom out of her wits.

One night, after having gone missing for a short while, Dad sneaked up to the trailer and crouched under its open window. With the flashlight below his chin, illuminating his scary facial expression, Dad jumped up and growled so loudly that Mom shrieked. Then her hearty laugh followed.

There are many great memories of our family getaways. When I was eight, Dad took the family for a week in Haliburton to enjoy time at a lakeside cottage.

I woke up and saw my father, with his messy jet-black business side part and two days' beard growth. Later, standing at the end of the dock side by side, we looked out over the blue-black, glass-like lake.

Before our dive, Dad gave a motivational speech, which I think was more for him than me.

Three, two, one... Go!

It was the end of April and the water was going to be a shocker on the way in. After his talk he immediately counted down, "Three, two, one, go!" On "go," we dove in together.

The frigid water stole my breath for the first few seconds. Then I started to settle into my experience with every cell in my body vibrating.

Julie, who was about three years old, stood on the dock with Mom. As we swam back towards the dock about to climb up the stairs, Dad let me go up first. Stepping onto the ladder, he reached over and grabbed Mom then pulled her with him. Together they fell back into the water.

Mom got out about two "No's" before holding her breath in preparation. He embraced her all the way in. She started yelling and laughing at the same time. She even got in a couple of slaps on his shoulder.

Mom actually settled into this bitter cold better than Dad and I did. She took a short swim.

My little sister, Julie, was yelling from the dock at Dad as my parents swam back towards her. Storming away, she did not talk to Dad for the rest of the morning.

My parents taught us how much fun a couple could have together, often finding different ways to surprise each other. It was clear to me that through the many layers of their relationship, there was a deep admiration for each other. They shared a beautiful friendship and passion, which most people only read about in novels.

I learned later in life that when you find this, it does not make the relationship a cakewalk. Despite everything, witnessing our parents' love for each other still lay the foundation of hope within us. They also imparted to us that if we ever give up on this type of love, we may never fully recover, and may regret it for the rest of our life.

We cherished our times up north together. Nature quiets us, healing us in the silence broken only by the sounds of wildlife.

When we had the trailer, Dad always looked for that abandoned logging road, drove as far up as possible, and parked by the water.

Another nature adventure

Memories of these times ingrained within me a love of travel, nature, and family adventure and escapades. I recall how Dad organized these vacation destinations with little planning. It was part of the adventure. The spontaneity was part of our experience.

The Herstad Curse

Late one day Dad took Cyndy, Valerie, and me fishing. This was a big occasion in the Herstad family because of the "Herstad Curse." It was never said aloud. When we were up north and when we were fishing, the only person who could say it was Dad.

Dad put country music on the moment we got north of Highway 7 as we headed out of Toronto. It helped with our mood as we eased into the North Country. Although he never said this part, I think it helped cure the Herstad Curse.

What was the Herstad Curse? We never knew whether this fishing trip would end well or be one of those misadventures finishing on a sour note!

We got ready to go fishing, gathering our gear, and Dad checked to see if we all had our rods, the tackle box, the net and oars in the boat, in case the engine failed. The boat was usually a twelve-foot aluminum with a pull-start engine. We had to untie our shoes in case we capsized and had to kick them off to swim ashore.

"Here we go!" Dad started the engine and we headed for open water with the wind in
our faces.

He looked around the waters like a detective at a funeral looking for the murderer in the crowd. He was trying to get a feel for the lake and the whereabouts of the fish.

"Over there! That's the Spot!" Dad yelled over the engine noise.

We got to his first Special Spot, turned off the engine, and drifted into the exact location. His voice turned into a light whisper, "We're here."

We gave him our rods and he set us up, oldest first. All the while he gazed around the lake and then at us, nodding with wide eyes. We might have even got a wink. Our job was to keep as still as possible in the boat and never drop anything, as this would sound the alarm to the fish that we were in their territory. We stayed here for about thirty minutes. If we got nothing, he whispered, "Okay, reel in, we're going to try another location."

Again, we were in motion under engine power, looking for the Spot. Again, he strained his neck to listen as if the wind in his face was whispering in his ear about where the fish might be. He would turn his head this way and that to let the information in.

"Over there, that's it!" Again, cutting the engine early, we drifted into target. If we did not get a bite or a fish in thirty minutes, he gave us a silent look and reeled in his rod. This was the trigger for us all to reel in and move to the next location.

No more curse

We drifted to the third location and repeated the same series of events. However, there was a growing tension in the air now. There was perspiration on Dad's forehead. After another twenty minutes he took a deep breath and exhaled loudly through his nostrils. As he looked around the lake, I saw that this was no longer a serene experience for him. He would shake his head from side to side.

We would be thinking, "Oh no, not again." But no one would utter this. A few minutes later, we heard him say, "Son of a bitch."

The first one was whispered.

The second was full volume. We could not let him see us laugh.

Shaking his head vigorously, Dad looked at us kids and said the words we were waiting for. "Yep! It's the Herstad Curse!"

Pulling away, we headed in to camp while he rethought his strategy.

The following day on our next trip, things went differently. This time, we were trolling for fish. For non-fisher people, this is when you put your lure out behind the boat with a cast, and then the engine power moves you and your bait around the lake. This way you cover more ground on an unfamiliar lake.

Out on our fifth pass of the lake, success! Cyndy got a hit. A big one. "Everyone reel in!" Dad yelled, cutting the engine. This stopped the possibility of fishing lines getting tangled when someone had a fish on. We reeled in and let Dad help Cyndy with the net. She reeled the fish all the way into sight and it was beside the boat.

"Lake trout and a dandy, Cyndy," Dad yelled. But before he could get the net under the fish to hoist him up, with its huge flipping tail, the fish broke the line and bolted deep.

There was deafening silence on the boat as we watched the fish making its fast escape. After another one-hundred-and-eighty-degree stare at the lake, Dad plopped down.

"Son of a bitch," he said.

Of course, I tightened my mouth to be sure nothing came out, making no eye contact with him. He did not like us noticing his frustration.

After a few seconds he took a few more breaths then said, "Okay, we found out where they are. It's getting late, so we'll head home for dinner. Put your rods down in the boat."

We called it fishing. We should have called it catching!

These family fishing trips were more proof that the country music Dad put on the car radio did nothing to cure the Herstad Curse. Oh, did I say that out loud?

Curse? What curse?

Mini-Bike Heaven

Dad bought me a mini-bike. It had a yellow tube frame with a pull-start lawn mower engine.

I had hinted casually and often about my friend who had a small motorcycle. David had an 80-CC Suzuki half road/half dirt bike. I spent a weekend at David's home and had so much fun taking turns riding his bike through the fields. Well, I was successful with planting the seed.

Dad did buy me a mini-bike.

The way he set it up was coming home early from work one evening, rounding up the family, and heading to the conservation authority park, which was a half mile south on 2nd Line West. In the park, he said he had to show us something, and we followed him to the river. When we reached the river, he announced that he forgot something in the car.

He ran back out of sight, and we stood looking around, admiring the flowing river.

All of a sudden Dad raced by us with this mini-bike. He had hidden it in the trunk of his car. He had no helmet on his slicked black hair. He wore his dress shoes, suit pants, and a white dress shirt opened at the neck, and his tie flew madly behind him in the wind. With a huge smile, he yelled over the roaring engine, "*Look at this thing go!*" as he flew by.

Sometimes his delivery was absolutely perfect! "Zeek, this is for you," he yelled, using his

favourite nickname for me.

I was totally surprised and could not wait for him to get off the bike so I could ride it.

The bike was called a "L'il Indian."

We took turns riding before the setting sun sent us home. We drove home and pulled the bike out from the back of Dad's car.

As I wheeled it into the garage, he said, "Now, if I ever see you on the road with that bike, it will be sold immediately. Do you understand?"

I rode that bike through all the fields within five miles of our home in every direction. I rode along the river, through the cornfields, and even visited David. We rode together, following each other through those same hydro fields where I had shared his bike with him.

Dad did well by me!

Chef Jerry

Early one evening on his way home from work, Dad dropped into the Port Credit Legion. There he met Jerry Sheridan, who was suffering through a tragic time.

Jerry had owned a restaurant business in Toronto and for financial liability reasons he had put all his assets in his wife's name, including their house.

The business failed and he was now working as a head chef at Toronto's Royal York Hotel. Earlier on the night my father met him, Jerry had gone home to discover that his wife had sold the house and all its contents to a new owner. She had gone back to Scotland. All she left him was the dog.

Dad called home before leaving the legion and asked Mom to prepare some food for him and a guest he was bringing home. He told Jerry he could stay with us until he sorted out his next steps.

I awoke the next morning to see a huge Great Dane bounding down the hall towards me. He seemed as large as a horse. I had to press myself up against the wall as he passed me. "Don't worry, dear, that's Brutus and he's with a gentleman who'll be staying with us for a while," Mom said from the other end of the hallway. "The man's name is Jerry and he's in the kitchen cooking us a wonderful breakfast."

Down the hallway towards the kitchen, I heard Mr. Sheridan telling Mom a story in his thick Scottish accent about how Brutus got into a big fight with two dogs the day before. Had Brutus picked up on Jerry's turmoil and taken it out on the neighbour's dogs?

We learned that when calling Brutus by name, we had to deliver it with that same heavy, Scottish accent to get his attention. Brutus followed Mom around the house all day. Whenever, wherever Mom sat down, he put his big head on her lap.

Mom had a calming nature, and it was easy to see her effect on big "Brrru-iss!" and on his owner.

Chapter 3

Dad's Legacy

Where's Dad?

It was 1973 and at the early age of forty-two, Dad was dealing with his heart problems and, I think, facing the realization of his own life and his mortality. It was shortly after his first heart surgery. He made a decision to leave us. He headed out to travel across Canada and stayed with friends and relatives along the way.

I do not remember him saying goodbye.

I was deeply saddened and so were my sisters. I was sad for myself. Why would he leave? How much could we have meant to him? It saddened me more deeply for my mother, raising four children and taking care of her ailing husband.

Because of this deep sadness we were all experiencing, during those months when my friends talked about their fathers, I would avoid these conversations.

While he was gone, we received birthday cards from him. Julie received a cartoon rendering of Dad drawn by some artist he must have crossed paths with on his travels.

We could not understand this.

Later, Mom told me that Dad's biggest fear was that he knew he would not be there beside us at our weddings to see us walk down the aisle or see our own children born. She explained that these

Dad's journey

thoughts haunted him. The last time the entire family went camping before he left, she would awaken to see him sitting up in bed, staring out the back of the trailer. Mom said, "Tom, I never had to ask him what he was thinking. I already knew."

Our Move to 2nd Line West

After he left on this trip, Mom did not accept his decision to leave us at all. I could not tell how mad or sad she was, as she kept it hidden. She was able to move us from that home to an investment property we had in the country. This move happened quickly. Mom called all her friends and her sister Cathy. "Let's get this done," she vowed.

We made at least twenty trips to that house on 2nd Line West. It was a beautiful, stretched-out four-bedroom bungalow with a big garage and tool shed on two acres of land. There were green plush hedges down both sides of the eighty-foot driveway, a full-size in-ground pool with diving board, and a pool house at the back left corner.

Golden hay fields were all around us. Some years there were horses in the north field bordering our fence if they did not plant the hay. The sun rose and set over beautiful trees and fields. The railway bridge across the Credit River was a quick fifteen-minute walk directly behind the property. I recall the echoing sound of the train coming through that river valley in the middle of the night and its whistle. It was magical.

Dad was away from us for a whole year. Mom was hurting, and was setting a tone for the rest of their relationship. If he ever returned to the other house, he would find an empty house, clearly understanding the message Mom was sending.

We loved this new house, which was free of memory, and now we could make new ones.

It was during this time that Mom had me go to the end of our long country driveway and close the gate at night. She wanted my father to know that if he returned, he would realize and see that he would have to earn his way back into our family and our home.

I found this particularly difficult. I wanted my father back, despite my conflicting thoughts about him. Each night as I closed the gate, I knew I was shutting him out, if he did decide to return.

We were shocked to learn that Dad did return to the area, directly entering the Toronto General Hospital, again with heart problems.

During this time, Mom received a phone call from Dad's former boss, Ron Sanderson of A. E. Le Page. "There's a man in the hospital who's preparing to die, and there's only one person who can save him," Mr. Sanderson told her.

Mom thanked Ron for the call, hung up the phone, and quickly made her decision. She got to the hospital well after visiting hours. It was quiet.

Dad recognized the sound of his wife's certain pair of high heels coming out of the elevator, clicking down the hall all the way to his room. When she reached the doorway of his room, she looked at him in the bed from the hallway. He stared at her, not knowing what would happen.

"Gerry, it's time for you to come home," she said softly.

That brought him home.

He was a different man, grateful to cherish the time with us, and to enjoy the morning meals when we were once again together. Sunday meals were again the main event in our home, as they used to be. Music, filled the house with joy on Sunday mornings again.

Margie and Gerry, Wedding Day, June 30th, 1956

Baseball Anyone?

I think it was a summer Saturday night close to midnight. My bedroom was at the back of our sprawling ranch bungalow home.

During the daylight I could see our in-ground pool from my back window through the honeysuckle bush. The pool was at the back left corner on this two-acre lot. Past the pool, there were hay fields as far as the eye could see.

On this clear-sky, full-moon night, I awakened to the sounds of voices and splashing. Some local teenagers had come to pool hop from the village of Meadowvale, about one mile south of our property on 2nd Line West. I got out of my bed and opened my sliding window further. As I stood there, trying to focus in on what was happening back there, my father bumped my unclosed bedroom door open with his fist and said, "Zeek, come with me." I followed him out of my bedroom and down the hallway towards the kitchen. He did not stop to put on shoes so neither did I. Out the back sliding glass door we went in bare feet, and as we left the single-man door to the sidewalk that led to the driveway, my father paused. He reached into the corner of this porch room and grabbed my baseball bat.

I followed my father quietly over the next eighty-plus steps to get to the back of the property. From the end of our driveway asphalt back to the pool was about twenty-five walkway patio stones. As we got close to the wire-framed pool gate, my father stopped. He took the bat with two hands and slammed it onto a patio stone. It made quite a loud sound. As he did, all of those boys froze and looked at him. Then he yelled, *"You boys want to play baseball with me?"* All of them looked in shock at my Dad. Dad then said, "Get your stuff and make your way to the end of our driveway. We are walking you out." I was eleven years old, and it was funny to see these older guys who I had seen on the school bus scramble to get their clothes and pick up their shoes. These were the older fellas who sat at the back of the school bus and heckled everyone who did not sit back there. Dad opened the pool gate with his left hand and rested the bat with his right hand against the top of his right shoulder. They each passed by us in single file. My father looked down at me and winked as we followed the last one of them from the pool to the end of our eighty-foot driveway. Nothing was said by the boys or my father until we got to where our driveway met the road. Then Dad said, "You gentlemen have a good night."

No Judgment

Dad's second heart surgery was to install a pacemaker. He shared his hospital room with a man named Don Canning. Don and Dad forged a close friendship, sharing common ailments and similar medical treatments. At that time heart surgery was in its infancy, and Dad's surgeon, Dr. Alan Steven Trimble, was our hero. He was a big ex-football player with big hands and fat fingers. Dad nicknamed him, "Nimble Fingers Trimble."

After both Dad and Don had completed their successful surgeries and left the hospital, Dad invited Don over for dinner at our home. Before Don arrived, Mom sat us down and told us that Don was a homosexual and he was coming to dinner with his partner. She said, "He's a good friend of your father's and we do not judge others because of their skin colour, religion, or sexual preference. Do you have any specific questions about gay people?" None of us kids had any questions. It was dinner as usual. As I write this I am reminded of how advanced and ahead of their time my parents were on so many topics. To have this type of situation occur in a home in 1973 was pretty remarkable.

Preparing Us

In those last eighteen months of his life after his return home, Dad did many things to prepare us. He would call home from work often on Fridays, and if I answered the phone, he would say, "Tom, put your sister on the phone."

Then he would ask them for a date: "You pick the restaurant or movie. This is your night," he would tell them.

It was a Friday. When I was in grade seven, he came to my school at 1:30 pm. The school secretary buzzed our classroom. "Is Tom Herstad in class? His father's here to pick him up for a dentist appointment."

In the office, I watched as he captivated the receptionist and secretaries with one of his stories. When he saw me, he cut the story short, saying, "Let's go, Zeek!"

I loved his nickname for me. When the school doors closed behind us, Dad looked at

me: "What dentist do you want to go to, Streetsville Glen or Glen Eagles?" We were going golfing!

He did this in the middle of Friday, when every single minute felt like an hour. He knew his twelve-year-old boy kept looking out at a beautiful, sunny, blue sky, willing the final bell to ring to start his weekend. Dad's timing was perfect.

Throughout much of our golf game, he talked to me, preparing me for when he was gone. He explained in detail my responsibilities and listened to my reaction to his words. He knew I tried hard to close my ears and fill my mind with other thoughts.

I could not bear to think about his dying, never mind discuss it.

It was during this time, whenever I stayed at a friend's house, I would lie awake at night wondering if my Dad was okay. Early the next morning, I would rush to the phone to call home. The moment he answered, I was relieved and was able to get on with my day.

He's Gone

Then it happened, and the dreaded loss cast greyness on us all.

On December 3rd, 1975, Mom and Dad finished dinner at a nice restaurant in Brampton, a suburb of Toronto, with Dr. Leroy Franklin and his wife, Pat. They met this couple when their son and

I played hockey together the previous year, and our parents had become good friends. That was also the year Dad coached the team. On this night, the two couples were celebrating Pat's birthday.

As they left the restaurant, Dad helped his wife into his new silver Monte Carlo with its half-grey vinyl roof. As he started the engine, he finished telling her a joke, and was still laughing as he put the car into drive and pulled out of the parking lot.

Mom then heard him hiccup. His head hit the headrest and foot floored the gas; He was in full cardiac arrest.

She instantly knew what happened and reached for the steering wheel. Steering the car out of oncoming traffic, down a residential street, up a nearby driveway, and into a house.

She crashed into the house at its garage. With bricks falling onto the car, smashing the front window, Mom grabbed Dad. She kicked the door open on her side and pulled him out onto the grass. She started performing CPR. When Dr. Franklin got to the scene, he immediately took over.

Mom stayed by Dad's side as the ambulance rushed him to emergency. At one point, they thought they had him as his eyes fluttered open and he seemed to gain consciousness. Dr. Franklin yelled, "We got him!"

But too many minutes had passed.

Mom stayed in the hospital with him. I do not know what she said during her final goodbye with the love of her life, but my guess was, simply, "I love you," one hundred times. Then perhaps for him to watch over us one hundred times. And then "Goodbye" one hundred times over.

He was gone, at the early age of forty-three.

Leaving that hospital as a thirty-eight-year-old widow, Mom knew she had experienced the full spectrum of a love some people may never know in their lives.

Her life and ours would never be the same again.

When my sisters and I awoke the next morning, our parents' bedroom door was open. Their bed was still made. When the phone rang, early, it was Pat Franklin, telling us that Mom was on her way home, and we were to stay home from school.

I was twelve, and remember walking around the house and sitting silently in different rooms. My intuition warned me; I was waiting for the trauma and grieving I was about to experience.

When Mom got home, stepping through the doorway and into the family room, she fell forward into the room. She blurted, "He's gone." As she hit her knees, she opened her arms. We ran to her, hugged, and cried together for a long time.

I remember not being able to cry. I stood holding onto my Mom, a numb feeling taking over my body. The biggest fear in my life had just caught up with me. My Dad was dead.

Mom held me close. It seemed like we held onto each other for an hour. Then she said, "Okay, children, it's time to get things done." We broke away from the hug, knowing that our lives had irrevocably changed forever.

The funeral service was at the small church in Meadowvale Village where, over the years, Mom had attended church on her own. The service was packed with family and friends spilling out onto the street.

Dad's Here

A few months before Dad died, he had wanted me to play for the reigning city championship team, the Royal York Rangers. I did not want to play for them. I was good enough to make the team, but I did not want to.

Dad had called the coach, and I accused him of railroading me. As always, I preferred to speak with Mom about our issues. Dad was very challenging to approach if our opinions or wishes were inconsistent with his desires for us. This had always been tough.

But they wanted me, and to appease my father, I went along with this. So, four months before Dad passed away, we were on our way to sign up with the Royal York Rangers. Dad was at the wheel and as we pulled out of the driveway, from the front passenger seat, looking straight ahead, Mom said, "You better tell him now, Tommy."

Realizing the seriousness in her statement, Dad pulled the car over, parked, and stared at me in the back seat with his burning brown eyes. "Okay, what do you need to say to me?"

"I don't want to play for Royal York," I stammered. "I want to play with Mississauga Reps with my buddies."

He rushed out of the car and went for a walk. When he got back into the car, I was grateful to hear him say, "Okay, Tommy, let's go and get you signed up with the Mississauga Reps."

I played hockey every Saturday; it was our usual home game at Dixie Arena. On the morning of my next hockey game, two days after Dad's death, my paternal grandfather, who came to stay with us, said, "Don't you play hockey on Saturdays?"

I said, "Not today."

Gramps said, "You play for him today. Get your stuff and meet me in the driveway." He drove me, and before the game started, the coach had the whole team honour my father with a moment of silence in the dressing room.

I scored three goals in that game. My coach was crying when I came back to the bench after each goal, and the crowd applauded me as I walked through the lobby on my way out of the rink.

I had never felt anything like this. I was an average player at the time. It was before the peak when I had realized I could really play. I always worried about my father when I played, seeing him getting worked up in the stands, his face red as he paced back and forth.

Whenever Mom was at my games, she extended her right hand up over her head, straight up as far as it could go from her five-foot-four height, and waved it up and down vertically. This way I could always see her in a big crowd, and that made me smile.

My Dad, on the other hand, supported me quite differently. He would yell three things at me, and I always heard him above any crowd. "*Skate!*" if the puck came to me and I could go with it. "*Move!*" if I was skating with the puck and ought to go faster. The third thing was, "*Get off the ice!*" if I had two mistakes in the same shift. This was so I could regroup, refocus, and think about what I was doing.

This morning, through my shock and my grief, I found freedom. Dazed, I realized it was the first hat trick of my hockey career.

The bittersweet irony was that I won the city championship that year with the Mississauga Reps. After the final game at North Toronto Arena against the Agincourt Eagles, I walked out of the dressing room and through the crowd. I dropped my equipment, walked halfway up into the empty stands, and sat down all alone.

I surely felt Dad's presence around me and relaxed into this emotion.

Mom watched me from the bottom of the stands and knew what was happening. She gave me a few minutes on my own, then she came up and sat down two seats away on my right, waiting for me to speak.

Sometimes sitting in silence is the best listening we can do.

Niagara-on-the-Lake?

Dad had willed Mom an acre of property beside our grandparents in Niagara-on-the-Lake. The acre was directly beside them, close to our cousin and aunt.

The year after Dad's death, Mom had orchestrated the selection of a new Viceroy home to be built on this property. She was going to move us from the country home on 2nd Line West to Niagara-on-the-Lake. If we moved, we would have lots of family around to support us. She had the Viceroy home all picked out and we had gone to see the Niagara District High School, and even met with the principal. On the eve of the final go-ahead, we talked with Mom at the kitchen table. Realizing that most of us were against this move, she graciously cancelled the move and we stayed at our home on 2nd Line West.

Mom took much heat from Nana, Gramps, and our oldest sister, Cynthia. They all believed the property should have never been sold and we should have moved there.

This friction lasted for many, many years to come.

Phoenix Rising: Finding Solace

Mom believed that we are spiritual beings having a human experience. This is why it is such a challenge for us. Many of us are not used to dealing with emotional pain, fear, frustration, anger, resentment, anxiety, and the biggest one, deception.

Witnessing how Mom dealt with the most challenging times of her life made my respect for her grow a hundredfold. She dug herself up from within the ashes through her own resolve and faith. It was torture to witness it, but I have learned a lot from it.

After Dad passed, Mom was devastated. She was drowning in grief for him while going through life, trying to keep the house and financial commitments going, all the while still helping others along the way. Dad had not left much in the way of life insurance. He had told her that he would load up on insurance when he felt it was close. But he never got around to doing this. On top of that, some friends had borrowed money from Mom from that insurance money and did not pay it back.

During this time, Mom started drinking at night. I watched her struggle, unable to help. Her grief was pulling her to self-medicate with alcohol. She would complete all the day's chores, make the next day's lunches, and descend into the basement living room, drinking while playing the old songs my parents had played together on the hi-fi. Vikki Carr's, "It Must Be Him" is the song I remember most of all the songs she played.

Homecoming

That winter Mom and I attended a Mississauga Rep. hockey team party. It was held at the home of one of my teammates, Dion. The home of the couple who were with my mother and father the night Dad died. Dr. Franklin and his wife, Pat, invited everyone over to their house after our usual noontime Saturday home game at Dixie Arena.

It was a snowy winter night as we arrived and parked on the street with the other cars. After entering the home at the main front door, we all milled around on the main floor of the house as more people arrived. Soon the party was split up, kids upstairs and adults in the basement. Before the decision was made to split it up, I will say that I noticed the parent couples treated my mother different now. I remember wondering why. Was it because she was not a part of a couple anymore, a possible threat? I made my way upstairs to the upper-level TV room. I stayed there with the other ten kids for about an hour. I made my way down into the basement to check on Mom.

Mom was always the first dancer in our home when the hi-fi was playing. Our parents taught us to love all types of music. On this night when I got to the basement, I saw her standing against the wall alone with a drink in her hand. The music was loud. I went to her and asked her to dance. We danced to the song "Low Rider" by the band War, and another song. Then I went back upstairs to the kids' gathering. Later that night, as we were at the front door trying to find our shoes in the mound of footwear, the couple hosting seemed to be rushing us out. I got the impression that one of the wives was jealous. I helped Mom to the car as she'd had too much to drink. Once we both got in, she drove to the end of the street, meandering between the curbs. The wipers were going back and forth as it was still snowing. I asked her to stop the car. She did not pull to the side of the road, she just stopped in the middle of the road. It was a residential road, so there was no traffic. I helped her get out of the driver's seat, then around in through the passenger door, into the seat. I grabbed her seat belt, pulled it across her chest, and fastened it. A man shovelling snow watched us from afar. Based on his reaction (he started walking towards the car), I wanted to get going quickly. I closed Mom's door, made my way around to the driver seat, and jumped in. The car was still running. I adjusted the seat forward, put it into drive, and pulled away. I remember thinking to myself, "This driving is not much different from our big sit-down lawn mower." I drove us home as she profusely apologized to me and spoke to our father, asking him for help. Her eyes were closed the entire time as she spoke all this out. She then passed out against the window of the passenger door about ten minutes into our thirty-minute drive home.

When we got back, I woke her up, helped her out of the car, along the driveway, up the steps, and into the house. I sat her in a kitchen chair, then took off her shoes and walked her down the hallway to her bed. She took off her jacket and laid in her clothes on her left side on top of the bedspread. I covered her with a throw from her reading chair and made my way to my bedroom. I have never told anyone this story until now. I knew it was an important secret I had to keep to myself. This story could never make its way through our family to our grandparents. I was fourteen years old.

During this period, one of the hardest moments of my teenage life was coming home late, anticipating hearing that old music as I opened the sliding glass door. I remember the horrible, sad feeling as I went downstairs, and on many occasions, tried to convince and help my mother to get to her bed.

The worst experience was the first time I could not coax her to bed. That flight of stairs was the longest I have ever climbed, having to leave Mom there on the floor while the music continued playing. I remember pausing three steps from the top of those stairs to make sure I could leave her there.

Lots of Room

When I was fifteen, my mother met a lady at one of my lacrosse games. I played on the same team as her son. Bernice became one of Mom's close friends. She shared with Margie her plan to leave her troubled marriage, but she had no place to go. Knowing that Bernice had made her decision to leave, Mom invited her to stay at our house. "You can stay as long as you need."

Knowing her backstory, Margie did not want her waiting to find a place. Sooner was definitely better than later. We turned our basement TV room and bar area into a double bedroom for Bernice and her daughter, Dawn. Bernice's son, Craig, shared my room with me. They lived with us for eight months, until Bernice found the right place for them.

During this time, eighteen-year-old Dawn became pregnant. Her parents were pushing her to have an abortion.

Mom never weighed in on this situation until the morning Dawn's father was about to pick her up to go for the abortion. Waiting in the kitchen in a rare moment alone with Mom, Dawn asked her what she should do.

Mom said, "It's your decision, dear, and I will support you with whatever you decide." As Dawn expressed later, it was the first time in her life she felt total support from anyone. It was also the first time she felt respected and treated like an adult by an adult.

Dawn decided to have the child, and Mom pampered her throughout the pregnancy. Mom went out of her way to remind her to sit down and rest, and would find her a spot and arrange the pillows properly for Dawn. Dawn's letter as a response to us contacting her is in later pages.

Jackie

About two years after Dad died, Mom met Jackie Hamilton in 1978. He was an ex-Toronto Maple Leaf player and a member of the Stanley Cup team. I was fourteen now, and still getting over the death of my father. Although I do not remember where Mom met Jackie, I know that he was one of the NHL old-timers who played in a memorial game for my Dad at Dixie Arena—the same arena where I played home games—a month after Dad's passing.

Coincidentally, a picture of that game on the cover of the *Mississauga News* had captured Jack Hamilton jumping up on the glass from the ice surface, right in front of Mom in the stands. They are both in the picture. This stunt makes it look like a player is going to throw a bucket of water on another player and it turns out to be a full bucket of popcorn, which they throw into the stands onto the crowd.

After an unexpected, extremely pleasant and happy six-month friendship, which turned into a serious relationship with Mom, Jackie moved into our house with us.

I was surprised. I called him Mr. Hamilton, out of respect and as a defence. No one was going to take the place of my father. Yet he proved to be unfailingly warm-hearted, overwhelming me with kindness.

He asked me to call him Jackie.

He was white-haired, a comfortably round man, five feet, ten inches in stature, and was about ten years Mom's senior.

In the beginning, our fun began when he taught me to drive a car, throwing the keys at me when he took me to my hockey games. I learned to drive at age fourteen. He spent time with Julie as well, taking her to the Woodbine Racetrack to watch the Thoroughbred horses. It became his routine to get her a pack of Smarties on these outings.

Jackie loved his work with the Ontario Jockey Club organizing sporting events for the hired hands who worked on the back side of the track while looking after the race-horses. He helped me get my first real summer employment with the maintenance staff at Woodbine Racetrack, which I loved. It was a chance to drive all sorts of different types of equipment. There were all sizes of tractors, trucks, a Bobcat, and mowers.

Jackie also organized special social events all over the Thoroughbred horse scene in southern Ontario, and played hockey on weekends with the NHL Old Timer touring team. I was fortunate to tag along to these events and help out on the bench or practice with the ex-professional hockey players. This was an amazing experience for a young, aspiring hockey player. This man helped me learn about the game of hockey, always teaching me how I could improve.

Jackie was cordial with our whole family, including my paternal grandparents, Nana and Gramps.

One winter evening when Jackie was living with us, he came down to the tennis courts in the little village of Meadowvale. This was where all the kids and anyone playing hockey went after school to play and hone their hockey skills. There were no referees, just a "sticks in the middle, divide them in two, game on" approach. The hockey name for it is shinny.

After the game, Jackie was there to take me home. As I came off the ice he said, "Stay on the ice. I'll get my skates on and join you."

Jackie always had his skates and a stick in the trunk of his car. We were alone on the ice. He asked me for the puck and shot it down into the other end. "Okay, go get the puck and stick-handle past me."

As I came towards him with the puck, he dropped his stick on the ice directly in front of me and continued to skate backwards. As a result, I collided with his stick, lost the puck, and fell. Without a word he picked up his stick and threw the puck again into the same end. Again, he said, "Okay, now go get it and stick-handle around me."

As I came towards him with the puck for the second time, he dropped his stick directly in front of me, and continued to skate backwards. I ran into his stick again with the puck and stopped to regain control of it. Jackie wanted me to realize that when I skated with the puck, I must keep my head up so I could react quicker to what was happening around me.

On the third pass, I had my head up, and as he dropped his stick, I made a move to my left to get around it, and then I skated by him, gaining speed all the way.

As I passed him, he said, "Okay, kid, we're done. Let's go."

Jackie taught me one of the most important lessons a hockey player can receive.

Keeping my head up, without having to look at my puck, I could feel it on my stick with the different vibrations of the stick in my hands. Without this skill, I would have never been able to achieve an advanced level. Once again, my mother was helping me through her relationship with Jackie.

Then we realized Mom had been hiding a dark, dangerous secret from us all. She told me that as bad as things must have looked to us, she was in deeper trouble than we knew. She had contemplated suicide and recognized she had to take serious action.

"I remember praying to God at the pool late that evening," she told me, her eyes glazing over with unshed tears. "I asked Him to show me the way." Mom had gone to the pool at the back of our two-acre property. "I planned to take the bottle of pills before getting into the water. I changed my mind, but I knew the thought would return to me, if I didn't take some drastic measures."

The very next day Mom found her solace—again while helping someone else discover their own way—by walking into Alcoholics Anonymous (AA).

Mom told us that she was going to take the lady who worked at the wine store to an AA meeting. "I think Doddi has a drinking problem," Mom said with great concern. "I think this because when she locks up at night, she usually has two or three bottles of wine with her, and some days she opens an hour late."

We stared at Mom. We had too much respect for her to say anything about her own drinking.

Mom took Doddi to the AA meeting, and when she returned, she sat us all down at the kitchen table. She did not even wait until the tea was ready. She just blurted it out: "I'm an alcoholic! I went to that meeting and listened to those people talk. That's me! I will be attending these meetings and will not be home in the evenings. I will need you all to help out around here more and pick up the slack. I need the support of the members to get back to being a better mom, a better Margie. It's time to do better." She committed to AA fully from that night forward and was sober for the rest of her life. She achieved thirty-three years of sobriety.

I admired how Mom found her way out of her situation and how she did it on her own. An important part of her healing had been admitting to us her thoughts of suicide.

Having gone through her own hell, and eventually coming out of the fog, Mom went on to help many others with pure empathy and without judgment.

She sponsored many into the AA program and was the first to say "hello" and shake a newcomer's hand. Sometimes I attended these meetings with her. This was when she was chairing the meeting or if she was accepting a membership chip. I recall members telling me how welcome she made people feel, how she exuded class and understanding. Mom and her dear friend Darlene were known as "The Huggers."

Looking back at this three-year episode of Mom's drinking taught me that even though it was hard to do, you had to let someone go through what they needed to go through, after you have tried your best to help. It is *their* journey and you must respect that and trust that they will be ok. Mom often said, *"Sometimes you have to let go and let God."*

The strong soul that she was, Mom got herself out of alcoholism once she committed to making the change.

White Light

It is referred to as a spiritual awakening!

I believe it was in the fall of 1980. Mom had left a nighttime Alcoholics Anonymous meeting alone and headed home from the church around 9 pm. On this thirty-minute drive through mostly residential streets, she then passed a beer store. As she drove by, the big sign caught her eye. Although she had already made a conscious decision to quit drinking, in this moment, she realized that she still had a curiosity about drinking. Margie took that thought further, then had to wrestle with her brain with a desire to turn the car around and pull into the driveway of that beer store. The next thing she knew, the entire interior of the car was filled with a soft white light. She then heard a voice say softly, yet very directly, "Be Love. Be Love."

The next thing she remembered was that she was sitting in her car parked in the driveway beside our house on 2nd Line West. She had no recollection of the drive home. It was as if she came to, in the driveway of our home. She exited the car, rushed into the house, and called another kitchen table meeting with us, her children. "I need to talk to all of you right now. Come," she loudly called down the bedroom hallway beside the kitchen. As my sisters and I entered the kitchen, I noticed that Mom had a very peaceful demeanour. Her cheeks were a flushed pink, her eyes sparkling blue. She sat down and shared with us her experience. I remember watching her calm delivery of this event. I thought, "How could this be? What was this? Is it possible to have this type of experience?"

She never had another thought or desire to drink ever again. If I had to guess, it was as though she had done enough of the AA work on herself required to allow something new to show itself to her.

I will go further to share another thought. I believe we can break down our life into categories. Maybe there are three categories? There are things in our life that we know, and then there are things in our life that we don't know. However, I believe there is another part to this thinking. There are things *we don't know, we don't know.* This is where I file this event for my mother in my memory of her. I'll draw on a simple example to explain what I mean by something we don't know that we don't know. Have you ever listened to a song for years, maybe even sung along to the words, and then one day, in a time of struggle or challenge, you hear the words to the song as though it is the first time you ever heard them, and it impacts you? You did not know, you didn't know the song.

Mom's recovery also brought on more changes for us all, especially her relationship with Jackie. A big part of their bond was being drinking buddies. Now, having found her new direction, Mom knew that for the sake of her health and well-being, she had to terminate their relationship.

I loved Jackie. We all did, and we were grateful for him in our lives. We were all sad at their separation in 1980, but we supported Mom's decision and commitment to remain consistent with her AA direction.

The breakup was also hard on Jackie, who often came to my workplace, asking me to help him get back with Mom. Though I was so fond of him, I could not agree.

Jackie also kept leaving Smarties in our end-of-the-driveway country road mailbox for Julie at night. He then began to attend AA meetings, approaching Mom there. Mom's sponsor told me that Jackie was beginning to harass my mother.

Because of his actions, I had to address him on a level I never thought I could, or would. I had to ask him, with great respect, to please stay away from my Mother.

He did honour this, and it was three years later at my grandparents' home when I next saw him. He would drop in on them once in a while.

Why Cry?

Another friend in AA was a rough, raspy-voiced biker, Mr. L. Early one morning I heard him speaking with Mom as I came towards the kitchen. Before I got to the end of the hallway, he started crying. It was a purging cry. I stopped in that hallway, listening. Sobbing uncontrollably, he kept asking Mom, "Why am I crying?"

"You're now starting to feel," She said. "This is a good thing. Cry with me. Let it out, you're safe with me."

I peeked in and saw them holding hands together on the kitchen table.

Years later, when asked about his relationship with Mom, Mr. L. shared the following: "Margie helped me understand myself. If not for her, I would not have the life I have today. She helped me learn how to live so I was able to have a relationship with someone and get married. She helped me with my wife. So many times, she sat with both of us and held us together through conversation. She was the glue that kept us together. Margie was my Earth angel. I told her things I never tell anyone. And I mean anything. We laughed so much together. She was the total definition of a friend—so much more than that."

When Mr. L. needed help with his first home, after getting married, Mom gave them their down payment as a loan with no interest. This was another entry in her Orange Book (the book she recorded loans in).

Do Your Best

In 1979, Mom had the garage converted into an apartment to make room for Terry, an AA friend.

Mom had always planned to convert the garage for her father when the time came, but now this sped up her decision. Terry needed a place to live while starting a new. Terry had taken in the son of a past girlfriend. She was still drinking; it was not a good place for the child. Terry wanted to help the boy, and together with Margie, they did.

While staying with us, David stole my car, a 1968 Cutlass Supreme. It had a 350, rocket engine, with black-jack headers, turbo mufflers, wide tires on the back and a top-of-the-line stereo system with Jenson speakers and a 100-watt power booster.

The car also had a musky, leather, new-carpet scent that only antique car owners have a handle on. The fourteen-year-old David took it for a joy ride down the street when I was away for the weekend. When I got back home, Mom sat me down and told me about it.

She said, "You leave him alone and let me deal with this in my own way. Do not touch him." She knew I would have liked to address this young buck directly, but I agreed that it was her situation to deal with and gave her my word not to "touch" him. But at one point I did ask David to come outside. When he did, I said that I wanted to knock him out but had promised my mother not to touch him.

He challenged me back, "Okay, do your best." He riled me up, not only because he had taken my car. I was more upset that he would accept my mother's invitation to come into our home, and yet show no regard for the property of others during his stay.

Mom helped me understand that it was not his fault. He had never been taught to respect others.

Again, she helped me understand why people do what they do.

David was a high-strung kid with a sad early childhood, but he turned himself into a very interesting and accomplished adult. David followed his dream of welding, boat-engine mechanic repair, and renovation work. He was a self-taught, clever, figure things out on his own guy. He had a "can do" attitude, always reaching out to help others, which I think he picked up from Margie.

He travelled extensively, enjoying his free-spirit approach to life. He was also a tattooist who expressed himself through art, both painting and sculpting. He lived just outside Vancouver on the water in his own absolutely authentic floating barge custom home. He moored it at a marina on the Pitt River. My sister Julie became close with him over the years. Julie recalls how during a visit in 2020 with David, he walked past a big block of wood resting on his living room floor, awaiting his unique approach to sculpting. He expressed this to Julie while pausing to look at the wood with a heavy stare: "It still has not told me what it wants to be yet." I enjoyed reconnecting with him for the sake of his input for this book.

Sadly, David passed away from a heart attack at age fifty-three during the editing of this book. We were so fortunate to connect with him. Here is his letter:

"My life has had its ups and downs but at the end of the day it's all been good. A lot of this has to do with your family, for me becoming the man I am. And I'm very grateful for knowing your Mom, you, and your sisters. I remember the day you called me outside regarding taking your car and you told me you wanted to kick my ass, and I told you to do your best. I was a little shit, for sure."

Go Do Better

Once, Mom sat down and talked with one of my sixteen-year-old friends, Billy, who had stopped in to say hello. Very candidly, she admitted to him why she knew she had needed AA, and the specific circumstances of her decision. These stories must have compromised her ego, but by sharing them, she created an environment for others to trust her and openly share with her.

Billy told me later that day it was the most intimate conversation an adult had ever had with him. She had divulged things about herself that he could never imagine anyone revealing. She had most probably shared these things because she felt his inner turmoil, knowing he might need to draw on their conversations for strength later in his future.

Her intuition was right, again. Sadly, he still had to fight his demons.

He has drawn on Margie's memory for strength and, if asked, would probably say the best advice she had given him was: "When you mess up or make a mistake, make your amends, forgive yourself, and now go do better."

Sleepover

I met fifteen-year-old Brenda when I was sixteen. She was my first girlfriend. We had been together for a year, and Brenda spent lots of time at our house and was like a part of our family.

One morning Mom came in the kitchen and showed me a coffee cup with something in it. She said, "I found this in the basement this morning. I suggest you be more sanitary with your safes (condoms). Now go throw this away properly, clean things up, and meet me at the kitchen table. We need to have a talk, you and I."

In my hurry to drive Brenda home, which was thirty minutes away, and return to get some sleep, I had not been vigilant in the cleanup.

Unable to meet her eyes, I took the coffee cup from her.

When I returned to the kitchen table, Mom said, "You're obviously in a committed relationship and you care for each other. You're probably using the car to be together as much as you're using the basement. You may even be wasting money on hotels. I want you to know that I'm okay with Brenda sleeping in your room with you. But you need to do two things: Brenda needs to ask her mother for permission for her daughter to stay over and sleep in your room with you. If it's okay, then sit down with your youngest sister, Julie. Tell her that you're in a committed relationship, which means you're only with Brenda and no one else. Ask her if she's okay with Brenda staying in your room with you. If she says okay, then you're good to go."

Brenda's Mom gave her permission, and then I sat down with my twelve-year-old sister, who was also on board.

From then on, Brenda stayed with me whenever she visited our home. This eliminated the late-night hour-round trips to her house.

Brenda and I were together for over three years.

By my Mom approaching the relationship this way, she treated me as an adult, trusted me to make my own decisions, and supported me in the decision. She also sent a message of respect that would help my youngest sister prepare for her own sexuality. By involving my youngest sister, Mom allowed her to be part of a family decision.

Dream Come True

I received an athletic scholarship and attended Rochester Institute of Technology, RIT, in upstate New York. I played on the men's hockey team.

I knew, the previous year that if I got the right career exposure, I would be a success. I found that chance thanks to Murray Walker, president of the Oakville Blades, Junior "B" Hockey. He delivered the necessary exposure, and while Ken Moodie and Eric Smith coached me, Murray continued promoting me to the scouts. Mr. Walker understood that junior hockey was a journey and not only a destination. He also proved that he was a man of his word.

Looking forward to the future, with the scholarship as my ultimate dream, I left for Rochester in September 1983. This gave me time to settle in as a single man, and better prepare for being homesick. I was on my own for the very first time. I remember my complete sense of accomplishment and pride in myself when I moved into my dorm room, put all my things away, sat on my bed, and told myself, "You did it." I was becoming truly independent. My dream of becoming a scholarship athlete had become a reality.

I was going to get an education and would not require my Mom to finance it. She had enough on her plate, juggling life and the rest of the family.

During my first year, something happened to me that I had never experienced before. I was a captain and all-star on almost every hockey and football team I ever played on after age fourteen. This was always a part of my identity, something that I thought was a given. This coach sat me out of the game lineup four games in that freshman year. Brian Mason was a great hockey mind, but difficult, for me, to play for at times. That being said, he was someone I thank for helping make my dream of playing in the USA and getting an education a reality.

Sad and frustrated, I called Mom one Sunday night. "I'm not going to sit in the stands and watch my team play. When I was recruited, it was all china and crystal, but now he's giving me Dixie cups and paper plates. I'm finished with this coach. I'm coming home."

Mom said, "Are you finished talking?" I said, "Yes."

"I'm not opening the door for you. You're going to hang up this phone, get back on that team, and call me in two weeks." I had never heard her talk in such a direct manner or in that tone.

I got off the phone, sat down on my bed, and had to smile. I did as I was told.

The following year my RIT team won an NCAA National Title. I was a starter on defence partnered with John Hawkins, from North Babylon, Long Island, New York. I would have missed that and the lifelong relationships I continue to share with many from that team. Those four years were some of the best I have ever experienced.

In a regular two-parent family, Mom could have said, "Hi honey, make sure you bring your laundry home. I'll cook your favourite meal. Love you! Now hold on, here's your father."

She did not have this option, so she delivered the strong message herself, and with her delivery, she had my complete attention.

Mom believed we were all connected, especially with those in our lives. Mom used to say, if you haven't heard from someone in your life for a while and they come into your mind three times, pick up the phone and call them.

Barbie

I came home from school after my first year at RIT in the spring of 1984. Entering the house, I could find no one.

Dropping all my bags at the door, I went up the stairs and through our home to my room, where I found it full of women's clothing.

Coming out immediately, I saw my mother in the hallway.

She looked at me, and with her index finger on her lips, said, "Shh, come here. I need to talk to you. Your cousin Barbie's here. She needs that room more than you do right now, and I'm not moving her around. Now you're doing okay, right? You got your first year of university under your belt and you're on your way. Yes? Know that I love you but we have an opportunity to help another here. Now, you need to make a choice: the spare bedroom or the couch. Which one is it going to be?" I chose the spare bedroom.

Barbie was around my age, about twenty-one. She was an artsy, fun, and very intelligent reincarnated flower child from the late 1960s. She always dressed with such self-expression. She later went into the film industry.

See, Barbie was Mom's cousin Irene's daughter. Irene was the daughter of Mom's Aunt Mayme. So Mom saw this as helping, giving back to her Aunt Mayme who had taught her as a young child how to be a mother. Mom and Irene had not spoken for many years. Barbie had issues with her father and the situation was at a breaking point.

When Mom heard the desperation in her cousin's voice, she said, "Get her on a bus. She can stay with me. I've got her."

I also believe that Mom selected my bedroom for Barbie because it was beside the kitchen. When Barbie first came into our house, she would have come in with her stuff into the kitchen, because that was where most conversations occurred in our house, (usually over a pot of tea). After their conversation, which probably went into the wee hours of the next morning, Mom moved her into my room because it was closest to the kitchen and lay empty. Then she refused to move Barbie around, needing her to feel welcome and secure in our home so she could start helping her heal.

Smile

Margie made eye contact with a homeless lady at an AA meeting in Toronto the fall of 1984. From a very early age, Rosie had lived as a homeless, drug-addicted alcoholic, who lost all of her teeth due to a lifetime of poverty, sadness, and abuse. Yet when Margie said, "You're coming home with me," a warmth came over Rosie.

Mom brought her home, put her in the spare bedroom, fed her, and mothered her, although she was a grown woman in her forties.

Margie trusted and respected Rosie, giving her the opportunity to trust and respect our home and enjoy a family life.

I was at school in Rochester for most of Rosie's three-month stay with us, but while home for Christmas, I saw them together. I remember her constant nervous laughter, while she was always holding her hands up in front of her mouth.

I have never heard that much laughter in our home, Rosie thoroughly embracing Mom and her family. I think she was over-whelmed to be living in a nice place, and was nervous in this new, warm environment. She trusted Mom completely, knowing she accepted her as she was, and cared for her unquestioningly. It was heartwarming to see them together.

Only with Mom did Rosie not feel conscious of her toothless smile. Mom bought Rosie a full set of teeth, and Rosie smiled openly for a photograph for the first time in many years.

Rosie thanked Julie for sharing her mother with her, telling my sister how she had never known the kind of mother-child love she saw in Mom and Julie's relationship.

When Rosie left, she sat everyone down at the kitchen table and stated that our mother had given her two gifts far more important than her teeth. Rosie said, "The first gift Margie has given me is the opportunity to witness your relationships and feel a part of a family. I have never seen this before. The second gift is that I now know how to love myself exactly the way I am."

Margie had taught her the principles of Love, Care, and Share. Most importantly, she taught Rosie how to love herself just the way she was.

Thanks, Jackie!

I often dropped in to see my paternal grandparents in Niagara-on-the-Lake on my way to and from RIT. My route along QEW highway passed close to their home.

When I pulled into my grandparents' driveway and parked beside their house off of the country road, Rural Route 2, I was so surprised to see Jackie's car. He had stopped in for a visit on his way to Fort Erie Race Track from his sister's house in Toronto, where he was currently living. I still loved the guy and was excited to spend some time with him again.

Sitting together, we shared our fond memories, especially how he let me drive his car to and from my hockey games when I was fourteen and fifteen, before I got my official driver's licence. I remembered how he sat in the passenger seat, looking over his glasses at me, saying, "Okay, Scamp, drive the car!" as he motioned with his right hand and index finger, pointing onward.

After our wonderful visit at my Grandparents' kitchen table and a meal, I was ready to get back to Rochester, but my car would not start, no matter what I did.

Jackie graciously offered to drive me back to school. Gramps would take care of getting my car fixed.

During the drive, we had time to connect more deeply. I was able to thank him for all that he had done for me, in so many domains, especially regarding hockey. I shared my gratitude for him teaching me so much about the game.

It was beautifully coincidental that Jackie drove me to a school I was able to attend because of his help. We hugged when he dropped me off.

Many years later, I saw a sports trivia question: "Who was the first rookie to score four goals in two periods during a Toronto Maple Leafs regular season hockey game?" I am proud to say that it was Jackie "Ham-bone" Hamilton, December 4th, 1943.

Eric's Angel

The first time I met Eric Smith was in my second year of junior hockey. He coached me with the Brampton Warriors. This was before I played in Oakville. Our coach had just been fired in the first month of the season, and here I came down the stairs of the arena into the dressing room area. Eric sat on a bench in the hallway. He had a big sheepskin leather winter coat with a fur collar and a big beige Stetson hat. He was a big personality for sure. I knew our original coach was fired the day before. I walked past Eric and our general manager, Punch, and into the dressing room. Being captain of the team, I should have stopped and addressed the new coach before entering the room. He let me pass him and the team manager without saying a word. I heard Punch say, "Let me go get him." Then I heard Eric for the first time. In a much louder voice, Eric said, "No, I got this."

Eric opened the door to the dressing room with a thud and called out, "Herstad!" Everyone in the dressing room turned their head to look. I stepped over my equipment and made my way out of the dressing room. He motioned his head down the hallway, and we walked in that direction together. When we got far enough away from the dressing room so no one could hear, he stopped and looked at me. The weight of his stare had my complete attention. Then he said this to me: "I get it. You are showing loyalty to your old coach. I like that and respect you for your position. But let me be clear right now with you. You will never disrespect me again. As captain of this team, you and I have to be together on everything. Do you understand me?" I put out my hand and we shook hands.

Eric was an amazing, brilliant, and warm-hearted man who knew hockey and people, and he took no prisoners. I remember his large handshake. His long fingers overlapped the back of my hand. And he always put his other hand on the shoulder of my opposite arm. He looked right into my eyes, and I had nowhere to go.

Once returning from RIT, I volunteered to coach my old junior team. I did this to give back, to help those who helped me. During that third year of coaching with Oakville Blades, Eric was added to the coaching staff with me. Here I found myself coaching alongside my favourite coach I ever played for.

That year we achieved great success together. We made it to the All-Ontario Finals. Tragically, right after that season, Eric suffered a brain aneurysm.

On the way to see him at the Mississauga hospital, I stopped in to see my mother. We sat at the kitchen table, drinking tea. I felt compelled to ask her to come with me as I stood up to leave her house.

Without missing a beat, she said, "Let me go put myself together and I'll be right down, dear."

We got to the hospital and walked into a tension-filled waiting room. His whole family was there. We immediately saw Helen, Eric's wife, and her obvious distress. Mom came in with me to see Eric. It was obvious that things were terribly wrong with him. His eyes were scrambled, in torture, openly trying to fight. I took his hand and felt his struggle.

On the way out of the room, Mom stopped and asked me if it was okay for her to talk with Helen. Mom had met Eric maybe twice and had never before met his wife. Shrugging, I said, "Sure."

Mom went back into the waiting room and approached Helen. I saw them walking down the hall as Mom held her hand. When they returned, I saw the emotion and commitment in Helen's face, and heard her say, "You're right, Margie, that's what we're going to do."

As we left, I asked Mom, "What did you say to Helen?" Mom had told her that Eric was struggling to hold on for them. She suggested they all go into his room, hold hands, and express individually everything they wanted him to know.

This would let him know he could go. It would allow him to release himself. It also healed that family from past issues. "So there would be nothing left unsaid."

Eric passed 2 days later. Mom had facilitated his death experience and healed a family in the process.

I was able to connect with Eric's stepdaughter Lynda after she messaged me on Facebook during the editing of this book. I hadn't spoken to her in 35 years. Her message was simple: "Hello! Is this the Tom Herstad who was coached by Eric Smith?"

Lynda had been on my mind from the beginning as someone I might interview for this book. I knew she had married a US military man and moved to Hawaii but had no idea how to find her. When we spoke, it was another wonderful reunion with someone from the past. We spent time catching up on all that had happened over the many years since I played hockey for Eric. Towards the end of the conversation, I told Lynda about this book and asked if I she would answer a couple of questions for the project. She was all for it.

"How did my mother's conversation with your mom in the hospital that day affect your family?" I asked.

Lynda's reply:

"Our family was in turmoil. We didn't know what to do. Eric was attached to machines and the tension in our family was obvious. As a group, we were experiencing frustration, fear, and pain. He just wasn't getting any better. I remember seeing you, Tom, and your mother, when you came into the hospital waiting room area that day. I later saw your mother approach my mom and watched them walk down the hospital hallway together. When they returned from that walk, they were holding hands. I could see my mother's face. She was smiling and crying. It was the first time I had seen her smile in two weeks. Her whole demeanour was different. After you and your mother left, my mom called a family meeting. She said that we should consider turning off the machines and trust what would happen next—what would happen with Eric and what would happen for each of us was to be trusted. My mother suggested that we all go in to see Eric as a group. Some of us wanted to go in alone, so we all agreed that we would each have time with Eric individually. One by one, we went in and sat with him. We told him all the things we wanted him to know. All the things we needed to say."

Then she said this: "It was as though your mother talking to my mom that day had opened a space for our entire family. This new space was a place we could find understanding, perspective. A place where there was peace, hope, and love. Our family changed that day. We decided to turn off the machines and trusted that it was the right thing to do. Our family united."

I had a second question for Lynda: "How did that day change you specifically?"

She said, "Your mother's advice to my mother that day allowed me to witness someone responding to another out of a love that came from understanding. I have often thought about what happened that day. Witnessing that allows me to be aware of something in me. In my relationships now, if I think about saying something but think it might be too personal or too intimate to say, I ask myself if the thought has everything to do with caring and love; if it does, I express it. I think that these are the thoughts that can be coming from a source much bigger than us, from the divine. How would the world be different if we all took the time to notice someone, to pay attention to others and offer a comment or piece of advice that we know comes from love and kindness? That would be a better world for sure."

Dad's Message

I once talked with Mom about my older sisters, Valerie and Cyndy. We talked about some unresolved issues Valerie and Cyndy may have had with our father.

Mom said, "Ask your father to send you his words. He will come to you, if and when it's right."

Two weeks later, I was driving and had to pull over. When it came, the words rushed through as if I were a conduit, and I scribbled the words on a piece of paper pressed down against the dashboard in my car. This was followed by an emotional purge.

When finished, I found a pay phone and called my mother. She picked up the phone and said, "Hello?" All I said was, "I got it Mom." She knew immediately what I meant.

I told her the message, which came in a poem. It was Dad's reassurance to his daughters that he may be gone but that he had not forgotten them, and he would always love them.

Mom cried. "Oh Tom, oh Tom. Go, give it to them!"

Keep on Trucking Night and Day

True to her nature, like she had done since she was eleven years old, Mom worked wherever she could find work. She bought a van and drove courier for five years. She was up and out of the house by 6:30 am and drove all day, delivering for a rush and express parcel service across the GTA. Sometimes she even took deliveries to Sarnia and Montreal at the end of a full day. I remember once she took a piece of the Canada Arm from Spar Aerospace in Toronto to its Montreal plant. She was so proud of participating in the Canadian project, and for many years after this, she told all her friends about her involvement.

Three nights a week Mom also worked the night shift in the local arena snack bar, serving drinks and food.

Sometimes she laughed, saying, "If someone drove by our property, they would have no clue that the snack-bar lady owns this home."

This usually initiated one of her end-of-the-day, tired laughter sessions at the kitchen table.

She did whatever it took to keep our standard of living as high as she could, and no job was beneath her. At one point, she cleaned new homes at night before they were occupied. This was dirty work as the construction workers cared little for final cleanup. I helped her on many occasions. I managed the vacuum cleaner.

She also delivered Meals on Wheels for the last three years she could drive. This was after she read the book *Course in Miracles*.

Whenever she read a great book that impacted her, she bought extra copies and gave them to people she thought could benefit by reading it. She did this with *Course in Miracles*, *Conversations with God*, and *Celestine Prophecy*. I remember how she helped in the community.

She used to pick up an elderly lady named Mrs. Tracy for Church on Sundays in the Village of Meadowvale. Mrs. Tracy could not drive and had difficulty walking. From what we understood, she had no family.

Mom was also a member of the Mississauga Board for Parkinson's, and was on the board for two years. She helped organize events, especially the Walk for Parkinson's, held in Mississauga.

If you told Mom something great that happened in your life, she would say, "I am thrilled for you," and you would feel her vibrate when she said it. Her voice held such enthusiasm in the word "thrilled."

Healing Laughter

Many times, I remember seeing Mom at the kitchen table, and she would start laughing for no apparent reason. This usually happened at the end of the day when she was tired and was finally able to sit and rest. Sometimes it would be because someone said something funny to her. After the initial chuckle and a long pause, Mom would start laughing. Whatever spurred her funny bone set her off. She would start slow. Then more laughter.

Other times, it was something that happened, like her stumbling as she made her way to the table. She would laugh at herself. It would come slow at first, and then build.

Others would join in as her laughter became contagious.

She later became aware of a woman who used laughing as therapy and Mom referred to this woman many times in conversation.

She believed that laughter helped us eliminate stress and cleared emotional blockages, which could occur over time if we kept our feelings hidden or suppressed.

Chapter 4

Time for Understanding

"How can I better understand this person I'm having an issue with?"

If Margie had a problem with someone, she said, "I need to sit down and have a listen with them." She saw the problem she had with that person as her opportunity to better understand them.

Having witnessed this often with Mom, I wonder what this world would look like if others followed the approach of trying to better understand others, instead of wanting to give someone a piece of their mind, or sort them out.

The Light

If you were having a hard time and you shared it with her, she would say, "Put the light of God around you." If it was a very difficult time for you, she would add, "And I will do the same."

Being a generous soul, Mom forgave her mother for their past, and when Grandma moved to Niagara Falls, mother and daughter rekindled their relationship. Mom always took us to see Grandma when we were near the Niagara Falls area.

Grandma's Loss

One of the most difficult times Mom had to deal with was when Grandma got gangrene in her right leg from lack of circulation.

At the hospital, she had to convince her mother to agree to surgery to remove her right leg. My mother told me, "Tommy, I said a prayer before I went in to see her. I told her the circumstances, held out my hand, and said that we'd get through this together."

Grandma took her hand in agreement. They moved forward with the surgery.

Almost a year later, while at school in Rochester, I called home and Valerie told me that Mom went to Niagara Falls to see Grandma in the hospital.

Grandma was in and out of hospital, but I knew somehow this time was different; she was in intensive care. I knew it was where I had to be, so I asked my hockey coach if I could miss practice that day, and made the two-hour drive to the hospital.

I sat in the waiting room and when Mom saw me, we needed no words between us. We just held each other tightly while she cried. She whispered in my ear, "Thank you for coming."

I will always remember and cherish this bittersweet moment. Being there for our loved ones when they need us most is a precious moment.

The next day my Grandma passed away.

Surrounding Bubble

In 1982, Margie went to stay with our Aunty Cathy and her family to help provide in-home care for her brother-in-law, Beldon. She stayed with them, caring for him until his last moments, when he passed away in his own bed. This was another bonding time for our mother and her youngest sister, rallying and working together to make this happen for Uncle Beldon. He wanted to stay in his home to the end.

During her stay, she had an issue to deal with. Many of the Bessey family were smokers. Mom said that to deal with this, she visualized a bubble surrounding her wherever she went. She said that after she figured this out, the smoke did not affect her anymore.

Mom also went to stay with our grandfather and grandmother, Dad's parents, caring for Gramps the last weeks of his life. She helped coach our Nana and all of us through the process. Gramps would even allow her to change him towards the end when he was too weak. He looked at her with such adoring eyes, filled with grati-tude. With her help, he spent his last days in his own bed instead of in a hospital, passing away in his home of forty years with all of us around him. I remember her whispering, "It's your turn, Tom. Go and say what you need him to know before he goes."

I told him that I would always remember him and would think of him when I had to make difficult decisions. Mom had coached our grandmother on how to release him, to let him go by telling him she was going to be fine. We were there for her and he could go.

Nana delivered this message lying with Gramps on his bed. It was the first time I ever saw my grandmother kiss my Gramps. He was gone a couple of hours later.

Grampa

Grampa, Margie's estranged father, who had left his young fam-ily to pursue work, had continued sending money home, but never returned. Mom had not seen him since she was five years old. After my parents got married, my father had discovered that Grampa had moved to Toronto years earlier.

Dad went and found him, brought him home, and told his wife to go and talk to her father. After many conversations with Dad, Mom had accepted this turn of events. As she sat with her father, the healing for their relationship had begun.

After Dad passed, Grampa, my mother's Dad, came every year from his home in Boston to stay with us for two weeks in the summertime. He would do all the chores during his stay. He could find and fix whatever needed attention.

Grampa, always there for Mom

Grampa came to live with Mom full-time for the last ten months of his life. She set him up in her spare bedroom and got him a big TV with a satellite dish to ensure he could always, find a baseball game to watch. He loved his baseball, especially the Boston Red Socks.

Mom coached him through his death, and they completed all that needed to be said.

After he passed, our whole family got together.

I remember dancing with Mom to a song by Roch Voisine called, "I'll Always Be There."

I felt her vibrating in my grasp. We looked at each other and no words were required. We danced together, knowing this was now her song between her father and her as tears streamed down our cheeks. This was a moment I will always hold close to my heart.

Annabelle

Auntie Ann was Mom's oldest sister. She was beautiful, slender, and blonde. Growing up they had lots of fun together, as they both loved to dance and were quite the pair wherever they went.

Annabelle habitually picked the bad boys. She ultimately ended up marrying one.

This man was a bright and motivated entrepreneur, but had a wandering eye and a playboy demeanour. Their horse farm was full of adventure and her household was an inviting, great place to spend time with my cousins, Greg and Danny. I spent much time there over summer vacations.

Among my fondest memories growing up were times we would visit Auntie Ann. She was so much fun with her big poodle dogs named Foo Foo and Fee Fee. A great moment to behold was when our Auntie Ann first opened the door and saw my Mom, her sister.

They would laugh and look at each other until they would be in tears and so tired of laughing that they had to sit down. The whole time they were laughing they would be bringing packages in and handing bags to each other. We would all end up laughing with them.

Unfortunately, Auntie Ann's marriage was suffering. I remember one weekend when I was staying over, my uncle came home late for dinner. He demanded food and sat down with us. The obvious tension was uncomfortable. At one point, my uncle threw the food against the wall and yelled, "You're crazy!" several times. He stood up and left the house.

They would later separate and divorce. The divorce devastated Auntie Ann. She started showing signs of schizophrenia. I recall the time Mom and I visited my other aunt, Auntie Cathy, in Niagara

Falls. We responded to a call from the police, Auntie Ann was at the local shopping plaza.

When we arrived, Mom quickly spoke with the police and then went to Auntie Ann in her car. She was clutching the steering wheel and having a violent conversation with a character residing on her right shoulder and another on her left—perhaps Auntie Ann's devil and angel alter egos?

Eventually, Mom calmed her sister so that she left her car and came with us. We took her home and waited for Mom to calm and soothe Auntie Ann for what felt like hours.

Years later, Auntie Ann was found dead at the bottom of the stairs in her town-house.

I was sick and could not attend the funeral for our beautiful aunt.

After the funeral, Mom said that she had to brace herself before entering her sister's house. She had suspicions about how her sister had met her early death. When Mom shook our uncle's hand at the funeral home, the physical contact confirmed it for her. Her inner core shook with the negative vibes coming from her ex-brother-in-law. Mom said that at that moment she felt great sadness.

"I knew there was nothing I could do and that I have to let it go now," she told me later, "It's not my place to judge another. But when I touched his hand, I felt something really wrong."

Chapter 5

Mom's Effect

Letter from Dawn

For Margie, Tom, Cyndy, Val, Julie, Friends, and Me...

Many years have passed since my first memory of Margie. Holding back my tears, my emotions run so deep for Margie and her family. I'll never forget this time in my life, and about what Margie had taught me, shown me, and given me.

In 1976, my youngest brother played sports with Tom. I believe the universe took hold and brought our two families together. My mother was trying to find herself after her divorce, and Margie was recently widowed. The two became instant friends. Soon, Margie offered her home to my Mom and my younger brother, Craig. Without hesitation, Tom shared his bedroom with my brother. The two were inseparable and they looked so much alike they could easily pass as brothers. Margie offered the space in the cozy basement for my Mom. I soon followed. With my parents' divorce, my life was a total scramble. Margie welcomed me with open arms, as did Cyndy, Val, Tom, and Julie.

During my rocky relationship with my boyfriend, I found out I was pregnant, at eighteen. At the news, I was pressured to have an abortion, but of course, I decided to keep my child. Margie did not have too much to say, but when we had a moment alone, she told me not to worry, that everything was going to be okay. "No matter what you decide to do, I'll be here for you and you can stay here as long as you want or need." There were never any "do's" and "don'ts."

She gave me the confidence I needed and I knew that my decision was the right one. While it took my Mom a while to accept it, until my son was born that June in 1977, Margie guarded me throughout the pregnancy and beyond, always telling me, "You must take care of yourself, you have to eat right, and you have to rest." She would take my hand: "C'mon, rest here in this chair." Well, Margie's plush emerald green chair was fit for a queen and she was sharing it with me. To this day I have always wanted a chair just like that. It was so comfortable. Margie would put the music on or start a fire, telling me to just stay there.

I found great comfort there. I felt secure, no longer afraid.

It was the first time I knew what "home" meant and I have never been able to recreate the ambience.

The kitchen was always full of great food, huge spreads, and endless laughter.

Margie's great big smile filled the room so much it could burst; sometimes full of the spirits of the liquid type. It was great fun. She was quick with quips and matter-of-fact whenever she had something to say. Everyone listened; she just had that way about her. Anyone who knew her felt her trusting soul and listened to her guidance. She would leave it up to you to find the answers.

Margie was my guardian angel and she helped so many others.

Often it was just me, Margie, and Teddy, the dog, at home. The kids were off to school, Cyndy and my Mom off to work. I'd help with the housework while Margie shampooed that white shag carpet in the living room. Everything was always in order no matter what chaos might happen. So often, I'd call out, "Mom," and Margie would be the first to answer.

That's how it was. We were a family with two women and 6.3 kids.

My boyfriend was welcome in the home too, even through the storm of our relationship. Eventually, we rented an apartment. Many plans for marriage just did not happen. Soon after my son was born, I was elated to visit Margie with him. When he was just starting to walk, I visited her, and in her backyard, he took some of his first steps. I have a picture of it.

One Mother's Day, a couple years later, driving to see my Mom with my two small kids in the back, I had a car accident. My mind was full of utter fear and darkness. I had crashed into a brick wall trying to avoid a reckless driver.

Thank God, the kids were okay, but I was bleeding from my head and my knees, after hitting the dashboard. My car was a wreck. No one was around. There were no cell phones at that time. But Margie's house was over the next hill; once again it was like a beacon of light and hope.

So I picked up the kids and walked to her door. I was dazed, still in shock, but when Margie opened the door, I could breathe again. As always, Margie remained calm. "C'mon in, c'mon in. Are you all okay? Is anyone hurt? Sit down, I'll make you a cup of tea." She brought me a cloth to wipe my face. I was home again. Margie offered us to stay as long as we wanted, or to drive me to my mom's, but instead, I wanted to stay with Margie until I was ready.

I knew that eventually I would have to take my children back home, but realized at that moment I was already there.

I don't think I would have been able to compose myself if Margie hadn't been close by. I'm sure that on her way back home, Margie took a deep, deep breath and thanked God that we were all okay. Again, she was an angel.

In 1984, I became a widow at twenty-five, after being with the father of my children for ten years. We were separated often, and hadn't seen each other in over six months, when the police notified me. Shortly after, reality hit, and I called Margie. I needed to hear her voice, to hear her tell me everything was going to be okay, and allow her strength to pass through the phone and onto me. I got through it as best I could, with two young children.

Years passed, but our distance was only geographical, as Margie and the Herstad clan were never far from my heart. I would run into Tom now and again, and catch up. The love was always there, always comforting and easily recalling the place I knew as "home."

In the early 1990s, despite my success as right-hand woman to the CEO of a large transportation company, I didn't feel fulfilled. I went back to school to become a nurse, to give back. Aside from the best reward of having my children, my job as a nurse fulfilled me multifold. Shortly after working in different fields of nursing, I found that my calling was visiting nursing, having the one-on-one, more personable approach. I did this for fifteen years.

It was Margie who sent me in that direction in my life, to help others, to pay it forward as she always did. She inspired me, and many others, too, to find good in oneself and help others.

After a serious back injury, I called Margie and asked if I could come see her. I needed to see her. She was now living in Streetsville. "Of course, dear," she said. "You know you can come here anytime."

We talked, we cried, we laughed; again, I felt home.

At Margie's suggestion I met her friend who had divine abilities, to help me find some answers. After the long meeting with her, I felt that same calmness and comfort I knew so well; I could stay there with Margie forever.

More years passed, and many times I wanted to see Margie. I missed her so much, but felt the years had passed and I didn't want to intrude on her new life. Big mistake on my part. I should have called. I should have visited.

Over the next years, as my health started to deteriorate, I needed Margie so much, trying to pull her strength toward me in deep thought and prayers. And I felt her.

In 2012, my daughter's new home was not too far from Margie's old ranch-style home. Driving on 2nd Line, I wished the house was there and that I could stop by, if only for a little while. Yet the essence was still there. The birth of my beautiful grandson recalled the time I was pregnant with my son, and the close proximity to Margie's home brought her to me so vividly, every day.

So many memories, so many happy times.

I love you, Margie. Thank you so much for everything you have taught me and all that you have done for me and other lucky souls. I'll miss you forever, but I know I can reach you in that special place in my heart, held there just for you so we can sit and have a little "talk" once in a while. I know you'll come to me whenever I need you. I now know that you always have been there. I feel better now.

Always,
Dawn

Darcy's Farewell

Mom had bought a couple of homes, and with the help of her second husband, who was a renovator, she turned them into duplexes and triplexes. These places were for those she was helping. I was renting one of the apartments in a basement of one of the homes. A single mother and her two children, Matt and Darcy, occupied the upstairs. Darcy, who had cystic fibrosis, was an exceptional young boy. I spent a lot of time with the two boys as they always came down when they heard me come in. At night, I could hear the mechanical thumper, which Darcy's mother used to clear out the fluid buildup from his lungs.

He passed away at nine years old, and his mother asked me if I would participate in his memorial service.

When I was preparing the eulogy, on the morning of the memorial service, Mom dropped in to see me. As I struggled with the ending of the speech for a message to his parents and everyone who knew him, my mother handed me a poem and said, "Darcy wants you to read this at the end."

It was the Mary Elizabeth Frye poem:

Do not stand at my grave and weep
I am not there. I do not sleep.
I am a thousand winds that blow.
I am the diamond glints on snow.
I am the sunlight on ripened grain.
I am the gentle autumn rain.
When you awaken in the morning's hush
I am the swift uplifting rush
Of quiet birds in circled flight.
I am the soft stars that shine at night.
Do not stand at my grave and cry;
I am not there. I did not die.

My sister, Julie, who sat with Mom, holding her arm during the service, later told me that Mom's left arm was shaking and vibrating. When she asked, "Are you okay?" Mom said, "I'm picking up on the grief of all these people."

There were over 600 people at this funeral. Every seat was occupied and people stood at the back, in the lobby, and on the lawn outside the church.

Baby Tanya

Tanya had come to our house with a friend of a friend one night. Tanya was a one-and-a-half-year-old little girl, and Mom had been asked to take her for the night, as her mother was going out dancing. The next morning, Mom sat down and spoke with Tanya's mother. Mom had felt there was something more going on than a night out dancing.

During this conversation, Margie found out that Tanya's mother was a stripper in a local nightclub and a drug abuser. She was having thoughts of suicide and was unable to manage her life.

Mom immediately offered for Tanya to stay at our home while her mother got things back on track. Mom jumped in without hesitation to help this toddler and her mother.

Tanya stayed with Mom for six months.

Unfortunately, during that timeframe, Tanya's mother committed suicide.

Margie was heartbroken when she had to give Tanya up to child services, who attempted to find Tanya's family. She ended up with her uncle in Quebec.

From Colin

I can't stand eggs! But one day at 2nd Line West, I walked in through the back porch door of the Herstad house, like we all always did, blood related or not, looking for Tom. He wasn't home...

Margie was making homemade egg-drop soup and was all excited about it, more so because I was there now to share it with her.

"Sit down, sit down, I'm going to feed you. You're not leaving till I do!" So to the big kitchen table I went and I stared at this egg, trying not to disappoint her. I was avoiding the egg, and she came over and said, "Oh no, you have to have the egg!"

Do you know I ate the whole damn soup, eggs and all?

Thought I'd gag, but I did it for her! Don't think I'd do that again, for anyone!

I met Margie at age eleven at Dixie Arena, playing hockey with Tom. Margie sat up there with Mary Tanti, the screamer! Margie yelled, "Go Boy. Go!"

Ah, that woman! That house! She was just love! And that house was unlike my own.

It wasn't just a house; it felt like *home*, like a family lived there. It was warm and welcoming as soon as you walked in. Not like mine, where no one was allowed over. Both my girlfriend Lisa and I felt so at home there. We felt loved and that we belonged there!

I remember us all hanging out downstairs in the recreation room, with Margie upstairs cooking. I remember that old piano, us playing pool in the sunroom, and swimming nude in the pool on a sixty-degree night. We were nuts.

The night before my wedding, we were in inner tubes naked in the pool! So much fun! My own mother was furious with me the next morning!

Often, I would drive over to visit, with only Margie there. Always a kiss hello, and a kiss goodbye; she never missed a beat that way. We used to laugh and think it was her way of checking for alcohol! But no, that was just her, lovin' on us.

We'd sit together and talk about life and how things were going for me. I could always talk to her. She'd throw her two cents in, but she'd hear me; she'd really listen.

"If you ever need anywhere to stay," she said, "you know you can always stay here. Pull your weight, pull some weeds, or mow the lawn, but this is home whenever you might need it!"

Bottom line, that home and how she was, informed me and modelled for me what I would be for my own children! Lisa and I talked about it back then. We were sixteen and seventeen years old, and we said we wanted to have a family and a home like that! And we did!

Love you, Margie Herstad. Always will.

Chapter 6

There's Always Room

Margie's calming nature: Mom spoke, cooed, sang, and hummed to babies and animals, instantly calming them, bonding souls with them. Often, we heard her humming around our home while doing daily chores.

If she noticed a blue jay at the kitchen windowsill, she would open the window ever so slowly and say, "pretty, pretty bird."

Animal Love

In addition to the many people staying with us, or passing through our family, Mom made sure we always had a dog or a cat, or both, at home. She said it brought more love into the house, helped make a house a home.

Probably the best of them was a female Samoyed puppy named Teddy.

Mom could not walk past her as a puppy in the window of the pet store beside Safeway, her local grocery store.

Five-year-old Julie thought our dog was a live teddy bear, hence the name. Mom named her Theodora, Teddy for short. A lovely soul, sharp as a whip, Teddy made singing sounds when she heard music.

She wanted to cuddle all the time.

She loved to run through the adjacent fields around our property. When we wanted her to come back in during her roaming times, we went outside and clapped over and over. We whistled, yelled her name over and over, and went back to clapping.

The beautiful fields were so thick, tall hay surrounded our home, and I would watch Teddy on the horizon, hearing our clapping and bounding toward us. We watched her jump above the foliage growth and then disappear. Every time she jumped, we saw a big ball of white fur. She was covered with burrs when she got back under the fence and into our yard.

One special thing Teddy did during family TV time was to rest on the living room floor while watching TV with us.

She knew she was not allowed up on the couch, but when she sensed a more relaxed atmosphere, seeming to wait until we all laughed, she attempted to get close to one of us on the couch. If one of us petted her, she slowly moved even closer to us. Teddy then leaned into one of our legs, heavily, tilting one paw on the edge of the couch.

After a minute or two, she tested us by moving that paw and part of her upper body onto the couch. The look on her face was of total joy and expectation, but also sympathy and sadness.

I still do not know how Teddy pulled off all those expressions at once. She did not try her luck too often, as if she knew it might stop altogether.

Teddy was smarter than all of us.

Whichever family member she was working on that night would laugh and sigh, "Okay, but just for tonight."

Getting the green light, Teddy preened and made her way up with her tail wagging. On her way up, sometimes her wagging tail knocked over glasses from the table.

If this dog was home alone, of course, she rested on the forbidden couch. When we came home, through the back sliding glass doors, we often heard "clomp, clomp" coming from the adjacent living room.

"You weren't up there, were you? You Dickens," said Mom. Teddy cleverly hung her head and withdrew under the kitchen table, until her next adventure brought her out.

When Teddy was four years old, Margie decided to mate her with a white German Shepherd who belonged to one of my hockey friends. They brought the male dog over one day and locked the two dogs in the back tool shed for thirty minutes. The happy result was five beautiful, white, furry puppies. I remember Julie and me getting off the bus to hear Mom yell from the living room screen window, "Hurry up! Teddy's in labour. We're having puppies!"

Mom found a large appliance box, and put it on the floor by her own bed in the master suite. She cut away a doorway and a roof off the box, and filled it with blankets, so that Teddy could be as comfortable as possible to give birth. This way she would be right there for Teddy, if it happened at night.

We ran into the house and down the hall. She helped Teddy with cleaning the puppies up. Teddy was tired and Mom cut the last puppy's umbilical cord. The whole time Mom cried quiet tears of joy, tears streaming down her cheeks watching the miracle of birth, as well as crying for the pain Teddy was experiencing giving birth.

It was truly exciting for us all to witness and experience the miracle of birth in our home with our deeply beloved pet. Again, this was part of Mom's plan, for us to share the births as a family.

We celebrated five puppies that resembled white, fluffy snowballs. It was beautiful to watch them crawl all over each other in the backyard on the grass, following their mother. I can only recall three names. There was Strutt, Snowball, and Rufus.

Utilizing word of mouth and a "Samoyed puppies" sign at the end of the driveway, Mom screened the people thoroughly while finding homes for the puppies.

One of these dogs kept coming back to visit our home at least three times after the new owners adopted him. They lived about five miles away. We guessed the puppy missed the home and the family he was born into.

Our Teddy lived to a ripe old age, and in her later years a skin condition caused her to lose most of her hair. What remained was patchy. Her tail deteriorated into a long, thin, pink bone, and the veterinarian assured us she was in no pain. It was simply a metabolic breakdown caused by age.

Mom found a sweater for her, and if it was in the wash, a T-shirt sufficed.

When you have an animal around, that you see every day and love to the stars and back, you do not notice the deterioration. Teddy had so much personality that her appearance was secondary, unimportant. Those who have seen the movie *Elephant Man* understand what I am saying.

I recall once walking Teddy in the park with Julie. Teddy stayed right by our side. Meandering through the park, we noticed people giving us weird looks and wondered why.

It became obvious when someone gazed at Teddy and back at us, probably judging us as unfit owners. Thinking, *surely something could have been done to help that poor animal.*

Julie and I glanced at Teddy, and for the first time, saw her through other people's eyes. My sister and I had a hearty laugh on the rest of our walk home, while Teddy walked on proud and strong.

This beautiful soul of a dog lived to fourteen. When Teddy was dying, I was in Montreal for the Grand Prix. Coming home on the Sunday night, I listened to three messages on the answering machine. All were from Mom, starting two days earlier, on Friday night, and the last message was Sunday morning. The first message was, "Teddy is in bad shape, call me." The second was, "Tommy,

Teddy is dying. Come when you get this message." The final message was, "Teddy's dying and she's waiting for you. Get here as soon as you get this message."

I immediately got in my car and drove to Mom's house. I came into the house and directly into the kitchen, lying down on the floor under the kitchen table beside Teddy. She then looked up at me, took her last breath, and she was gone.

We were all there in that kitchen; God love her that she waited for all of us to be together before she left us.

Perhaps she knew I would be the one to bury her, even though we were all overwhelmed with grief. I gently picked her up and carried her to the back of the property beside the pool. After digging her grave and thanking her for her life with us, I laid her to rest.

Mailing Birds

Our beautiful home on 2nd Line was one mile north of the little village of Meadowvale in the north end of Mississauga. Acres of fields surrounded us, and half a mile behind the house was the Credit River.

At the end of our long driveway, we had a big mailbox that hung out over the ditch for the postal service.

One night, some local yahoos driving up and down the street put a shotgun blast through the mailbox. The blast left gaping holes in both sides of it.

Why had we not heard this?

Before we could get the mailbox replaced the next week, chirping sounded, and yes, it was coming from the mailbox. Blue jays had taken up occupancy in it and had babies.

Excited about this, of course, we refused to disrupt the family of birds.

Mom delayed replacing the mailbox and had the local post office hold the mail for her pickup, until the birds were big enough to leave the nest.

After the first year, I reminded her, "Mom, how about replacing this old mailbox now that they're gone?"

"Don't be silly, Tom," she said. "They'll be back next year and that's their spot."

Henrietta's Back

After the house in the country on 2nd Line West was sold in 1983, we moved to Tannery Street in the small town of Streetsville, not far from the centre of town. Mom had moved to downsize and use the additional money to buy other homes and make apartments for those around her.

It was a blue sky, cool spring morning when a hen walked up our driveway from the road. Did she fall off a farmer's truck or walk over from a local farmer's market? Looking out through the kitchen window, Mom saw her coming up our driveway.

Going outside, Mom opened the gate to our backyard. The hen waddled through, authoritatively settled in, and made a nest in the back left corner of our yard.

Mom decided a fitting name would be "Henrietta the Hen," who now laid eggs and sat on her nest until they started to smell. Laughing, we had to coax her with bread to get up, while someone else grabbed and bagged the rotten eggs for disposal.

If we ever complained to Mom about Henrietta, she said, "That's her spot now and you leave her be."

Now, imagine this backyard. In the centre is an in-ground blue pool, ten feet in the deep end, with a diving board and slide and steps down into the shallow end. On the left sat the family-size BBQ with comfortable lawn chairs, with the pool house at the far back left.

The right and back had eight-foot-high privacy fencing dividing us from the road. On the left side, a wire mesh fence allowed us to enjoy the property view with the two huge weeping willows and the babbling brook that flowed through the property.

At our parties, if newcomers were not aware of Henrietta's presence upon their arrival, they might have thought, *What the %%$$! is with the duck, I mean hen?* And if they said it aloud and if Henrietta could speak, she would have probably chimed in with, "I heard her tell you this is my spot and you are to respect that."

She certainly made her presence known.

One morning, Mom stared at Henrietta from the kitchen window and turned to look at us sitting at the table. "Let's go to a local farm."

There she asked the farmer for fertilized eggs. Back home, we coaxed Henrietta out of that nest, replacing her unfertilized eggs with fertilized ones. Lo and behold, when they started to hatch, we heard Henrietta squawking in the backyard, realizing her eggs were breaking open; she was now a mother! She strutted around the backyard, proudly leading the pack and caring for her flock.

Much later, I came home one weekend from school, and Henrietta and her chicks were gone. I asked, "Mom, what happened?"

"Henrietta seems to have moved on. She was the soul of a pet I had in the East Coast when I was four. She'd gone missing back then, Tom, and I was heartbroken. I thought she stopped in here to say hello again. But, She may be gone for good, but you never know."

Chapter 7

Finding Our Way

Mom always supported us pursuing life as a continuing evolution. She encouraged us to always work on ourselves. This work included speaking out our problems with those we had issues with, being patient with ourselves when we did not know how to cope with a certain situation, as well as allowing each of us time and space to do that. She said, "You will always find your way."

Healing Time

Through a friend, Mom became aware of a course named The Forum, which was held at Landmark Education in Toronto in 1990. She sat down with Julie, my (then) fiancée Cathy, and me and said, "I found out about a course that might help us. It's something that will add to our life experience. I want us all to go do this together."

Of course, we all agreed. "Sign us up."

The message here, and throughout her life, is that our Mom was a force to be reckoned with, especially when she got something in her mind.

We all knew that when she wanted us to commit to something, it was right for us to do, together. We never second-guessed her.

My experience in this course was profound.

Through it, I was able to revisit an event in my life that I had still carried with me, deep within my subconscious. During this course, we were asked about our childhood memories.

I remembered the feeling of not being loved, when I was in grade three. That fall morning as class started, Mrs. Zebec had told me to leave, go home, and get a signature from my parents on a math test for which I received three out of ten.

I delayed showing it to my parents for two weeks.

My school was right behind our house, and Mrs. Zebec knew this. When I got home, I approached my mother, "Mom, can I get a quick signature on this test? I've got to get right back to school."

She said, "You know who signs those. He's upstairs getting ready for work." Slowly I went up to their bathroom. I knocked on the door and told Dad that I needed him to sign something for school.

The door opened slightly as I extended a shaking hand to give him the test, upside down.

He took it from me, then opened the door, enough for me to see his face full of shaving cream and slowly said, "Wait for me downstairs."

Downstairs, I waited, a nervous wreck. To disappoint him with this type of test score in school was lethal.

Coming down the stairs, dressed in his business attire, he said, "Let's go, Tom. I'm walking you back to school." All the way back he berated me. "We're not going to have a stupid kid in our family. This stops today."

I remember almost blacking out as he spoke, staggering in my step. I was living my worst nightmare.

At school, he marched me down the hall into my class, and asked Mrs. Zebec to come out for a moment. As I stood frozen in front of the class, all we could hear in his thundering voice was how

I was to bring home extra work, and he would be in touch with her weekly, until this kind of test score was a thing of the past.

Mrs. Zebec came back into the class, looked at me and said, "Now, you heard your father!"

As a child, I had interpreted this to mean I was not good enough, that Dad did not love me. I didn't measure up.

Revisiting this event, as an adult, I realized how much my father loved me, taking time out of his day to walk me back to school, and addressing the situation head on with me.

Once I recognized that his delivery sucked, my breakthrough resulted in me writing my dead father a letter. In it, I expressed how I loved him for supporting me that day, for showing his commitment to me, how I was good enough to receive all of this! I also said that I forgave him for his delivery.

I was able to read this out loud to Mom and Julie. Happily, those old feelings of inadequacy disappeared. I cried for my father while reading and after reading this letter. I had never cried for him until that moment. Grief was purged out of me.

I then realized that as successful as I had been in school since that day in grade three, I had never owned any of it, because in my subconscious mind, I was still that eight-year-old who was stupid, unloved, not good enough. Now I was able to look back and own my accomplishments in school.

I now recognized that my father had always loved me. Positive memories I had squashed from my childhood came back to me like a tidal wave.

I remembered the golf on that Friday afternoon. I remembered the coaching he did with all my teams. I remembered winning first star in the final championship game at a hockey tournament in Ajax, Ontario. I had just received the award at centre ice, and on my way back to our bench, I threw it to him and he said, "Great game!"

Today, I think about how many of my friends still had their fathers and may not have experienced this or shared these types of memories. I felt fortunate. I also felt complete with my Dad.

Once again, Mom had led us on the track of further self-discovery.

Know This

I went to my mother when I had to talk to her, to share my mistake. I had made a business deal, which led to a disagreement with my business partner.

Instead of dealing with it professionally, I did something mean to get back at him and was ashamed of myself. My sense of integrity was badly bruised. The intolerable burden had grown too big, eating away at me.

I had to tell someone.

I drove to her house and we sat in the kitchen over a pot of tea. She asked, "What's on your mind, dear?"

I told her I had to share something with her. She must have sensed the importance because she moved her chair directly in front of me. "Go ahead, dear."

While I told her everything that was on my mind, she did not interrupt me or react to what I said.

Her eyes remained glued to mine. "Tom, are you finished saying everything you need to say to me?"

I nodded, then bowed my head. She sat silently until I looked up at her. She looked me square in the eye, saying, "You could never tell me anything about yourself that would ever change my opinion of you. Know that I love you. Forgive yourself. This will open the door to your path. Now go do better."

With that statement, she took it all away from me. A piano-sized burden of pain and shame was lifted off me.

She healed me instantly.

Then Mom stepped away from the table and asked me if I wanted a cup of tea.

I left that day ready for my future, and also made amends with my partner when the opportunity presented itself.

Inner Voice

"Get quiet and trust your inner voice. Your inner voice will guide you." Mom believed that we all have the ability to know what to do in any situation or in any decision we have to make.

"You have an inner voice that will always let you know the right thing to do in your life. Get still and listen to that voice, then respond," Mom told us.

This can easily be understood with this example: You are grocery shopping and see something that is not on your list. You pick it up and then put it back. You wonder if you should buy it, but you do not. When you get home, you put away your groceries and realize you are out of the item you picked up at the grocery store.

Or, you are in the hardware store and notice a tool you have not seen before. You are not sure if you have one. You pick it up, study it, then you put it back on the shelf. Two days later, you are working on something around the house and you realize you need that particular tool you had picked up in the store.

This is how your inner voice wants to help guide you. By the way, both males and females can be the lead actor in either scenario. "Now, Quiet On The Set!"

Difficult Questions

When asked a difficult question to explain human behaviour or a complex question on many levels, Mom's response would be, "What would Jesus say?" or "What would Jesus do?"

Schooling Mom

Mom did not go to high school. In fact, she only finished grade six. So, in her forties, she took night classes at Sheridan College. One night she rushed into the kitchen, opened her purse, and put her test down on the table.

"Look!" she said, "I got eight out of ten on this test."

I looked at her and said, "What's the big deal? I know you're smart."

She looked at me, shocked and surprised. Did she not know her own intelligence and smarts? As I walked out of the room, I saw how reassured she was that she was capable of grasping the material and getting good grades. She must have thought that because she had not finished schooling, She was not smart.

This may have been another reason why Mom was a natural with children. She yearned to help youngsters and their parents to get off to a good start and get on the right track early.

Her Kids

After her courier days came to an end, Mom looked after children in our home. This childcare service catered to the locals in the neighbourhood. Mostly she had preschoolers, but also offered an after-school service.

At one point Mom had thirteen children in her care over the course of a day. Starting her day at 6 am and finishing at 7 pm or even 8 pm Monday to Friday, she developed close relationships with the children as well as their parents.

Many children came from single-parent families, and Mom often invited their mothers or fathers to stay for a visit when picking up their children.

Mom could sense if someone was out of sorts and she always wanted to help. This naturally happened over a cup of tea. It was obvious to me that Mom provided much more than strictly child-care for these parents.

During her childcare business, Mom established a time-out spot. It was referred to as "The Brown Chair." It was how she handled a problem with the children. The beautiful, brown Victorian-style chair sat removed from everyone in the bay window of the living room. With its hand-carved wooden handrails, velvet padding, and plush brown cushion, it was a chair for royalty.

It was adorable seeing from outside the house through the big bay window, one of the children sitting serenely in the regal chair. As bad as they might have been to deserve the time-out, they looked so darned cute and well behaved, sitting there quietly.

"The Brown Chair"

From Maureen Jenkins

"Sean, the Bomb" was one of the first children Mom took in for her daycare business. He was a stocky, blue-eyed, blonde boy who was a force to be reckoned with. His mother was Maureen K.

Although it had been thirty-five years since Mom had helped Maureen with her children, when I contacted her for this book, Maureen was excited to help and shared the following tribute:

Tears are rolling before I even get started here, thinking about your Mother. She was an incredible lady and I think about her often. It was a long time ago and I don't remember a lot of things, but those years when she was such a big part of my kids' lives will never fade.

Sean was a baby when we were first introduced. Our meeting was the best thing that happened at the time. I was raising him on my own, with Brian away a lot with his golfing career, and I worked part-time. Margie decided he should call her "Auntie." To this day, whenever Margie comes up in conversation, it's still "Auntie."

She decided when it was time for Sean to be potty trained or come off the bottle. I knew she meant business. As I was still young myself, I listened to her. He would kick up when I was leaving him, and she insisted I leave quickly and calmly, knowing he was perfectly fine the minute I was out the door. She taught him how to swim in your pool. I certainly couldn't have done it, as I can't swim myself.

Margie had less to do with Dana, my second child, because I didn't work when she was little. However, Margie was there when I needed her.

By that time, Valerie was babysitting. I'll never forget the day I came home to an empty house. Dana was prone to febrile seizures, and when I saw the bathtub filled with water, my heart sank. It wasn't long before the phone rang. It was Margie saying Dana had had a convulsion, Valerie had called 911, and they were at the hospital.

I remember how the nurses praised Valerie for handling the situation like a pro—something she had obviously learned from her mother.

Sean is forty-four this year and Dana is forty. To them, "Auntie" is the epitome of kindness and love! An incredible lady who certainly impacted our family and, no doubt, influenced those many others she touched because of her loving, nurturing, selfless, giving, and caring nature.

What a great thing you're doing, Tom, a true testament of who she was and how she raised you guys! She was so proud of you all and your accomplishments!

Looking forward to reading the book!

Love to you all,
Maureen

Lulu

Mom took in a teenage girl named Lulu. Valerie brought this girl to our home after they became friends. Lulu was nineteen and pregnant. She had a challenging past, and was currently in an abusive relationship and needed help. Mom had her stay with us until her baby boy was born. She had even wanted Margie in the delivery room with her.

Later, they made a self-written and signed adoption agreement confirming that from that day forward, Mom would be the new baby's guardian. Mom participated in the upbringing of that child, treating Warren as if he were her own grandchild. He referred to her as "His Auntie."

Mom helped Lulu with places to stay. As Mom acquired more properties, this young lady rented two or three of these homes as her needs changed.

Eventually, Lulu had two more children and Mom invested in a house for this girl and her children when she needed a bigger place. Because of their shared similar tragic childhood experiences, Lulu and Mom forged a serious bond with each other.

Warren was one of the first daycare children in Mom's house. This young lad had a hard time sharing his Auntie with the rest of the daycare children. Often, we would see him in the famous Brown Chair.

I remember my mother's repeated words: "Warren wants to be a good boy! Yes?"

Warren had many issues growing up and always found his way back to his Auntie to help him feel her love and acceptance.

Later, during his teens, Warren often visited her. He had even helped convince Mom how marijuana could help her with her increasing aches and pains associated with Parkinson's disease. It must have been fun to keep this very interesting part of their relationship a secret from everyone else. I guess Warren had a chance to contribute and help his Auntie in a way no one else could.

Warren had a brilliant mind. In his twenties he shared with me his unique poetry, and his rapping was as good as anything I have heard on the radio.

His handle was "Big Chief." My nickname for this young man was Rhubarb. He once sent me a picture of him holding a piece of rhubarb pie up to his cheek with a big smile.

He liked to present a gangster persona, but under that ball cap, rough-looking clothing, and his robust, hearty laugh, he was a mush ball with a good heart. He had tried desperately to put his past habits behind him and even completed four stints in rehab to the finish.

We drove three hours north together to his first rehab stay. We had picked up a member of AA to help coach him in. The consistent message this AA member delivered was for Warren to surrender to this new experience—give in, to this new recovery journey.

It saddens me to say that Warren passed away during the writing of this book from substance abuse. We were so fortunate to have interviewed him early in this project.

Here is Warren's tribute to his Auntie.

Warren's Tribute

My story with her would be its own movie. Auntie Margie means the world to me, no one could ever understand. Every time she hugged me, I no longer felt alone. She was like a mother to me. She showed me what love felt like. And she was *my* Auntie! No one else's. (Meaning, with their very strong connection, as a toddler he never wanted to share her with the other kids Mom looked after. After all, *he* got to sleep over, while the others did not.)

She taught me to visualize when I was little, to keep the negative feelings away. She protected me from evil. She took me to my first AA meeting. At first, I wanted to go to be involved with what she did, and to protect her.

And I'll never forget when she first held my son, she was full of pure joy, only way to describe it.

She's in my dreams a lot. She comes to me. I can talk to her.

Two days before they told me she had died, I had a dream about her; I was a kid and she was singing "Daisy, Daisy" to me in the pool. She was holding me and I was crying about something. She taught me to translate that to a visitation, like she had wanted to check in before she left.

But you know she's never left me, and I know that.

She's the only one who never does.

Warren's War and Peace

Long ago, I had prepared myself for the phone call I could receive regarding the end of Warren's life. But it did not make it any easier when it came.

At his service, I sat with my family, wishing I could hear him laugh one more time. I wanted to see him sitting by the window at Coffee Time and join him just one more time. I wanted to hear his cheeky way of trying to convince me to "lend" him money, just one more time.

During his off and on stays with me over the years, I felt a kinship with him, which allowed me to see him through all his trials and tribulations despite his bravado.

A month after his passing, Julie called me. As much as I was able to accomplish with Warren, she had done ten times more.

In her voicemail message my sister said, "Hey, it's me, I'm going to try to say this without getting too emotional, but I just had a big cry! Something extraordinary just happened. I'm on my way to work, on Highway 10 and the roads aren't good so I'm trying to take my time. And," she paused and then continued, "I picked up my phone just to see what time it was and a picture of Warren appeared on it!"

She paused again as she collected herself. "He looked like he was three with his bowl haircut, and he's hugging Mom."

Another pause. "But guess what? I don't have any pictures of him on my phone!" Another pause. "Was that him getting through to me? Oh my God! I touched the screen to make it bigger and it went away, going back to the normal home page. But I don't even have that picture anywhere on my phone or even on my computer! Anyway, I've got to pull it together here and go and be 'Smart Julie' at work now. I wanted to share that with you. Love ya."

Thanks to our Mom's teachings, my siblings and I were open to these incredible messages, which kept us aware of the spiritual world all around us.

Chapter 8

Family Homes

Tannery Street Home

Mom sold the house in the country on 2nd Line West in 1983 and moved to the centre of a small town called Streetsville. Years later, she told us that she knew she was meant to be there when she drove across the bridge in front of the property.

"Coming over the bridge I saw the sunlight break through the clouds, illuminating the house. I stopped the car, got out, and enjoyed the welcoming sound of the brook. Then, when seeing the two huge towering willow trees, I knew this was where I was meant to be." With the difference in property values, she was able to pay in full and have no mortgage for the first time. This home also had a pool and pool house.

The Pool House

This new home's pool house was converted into a two-bedroom cottage. Many friends and family members had their time in this safe haven, a step up and out into the world.

They would check in for a short time or a long time—a stepping-stone for many. It was a halfway house without the official title, if you will, for people needing a sense of belonging to a family close by, while still having their independence.

Consciously or subconsciously, they were coached out of that cottage by Margie and taught to gather their courage and move on into the world.

Bait and Switch

At one point in Mom's life, she had mortgaged a property to buy another house. The additional house was split into separate successful income units. Continuing with this approach, Mom accumulated five homes.

She continued to be a loyal attendee at AA and helped many people. She sat next to a man who seemed very nice. When she had talked with my Dad so long ago, he had suggested that she might consider a second marriage with someone who was a "Steady Eddy." One man appealed to her, and first they lived together and then later got married in 1991.

He was an aluminum worker and was doing the renovations until he got kidney disease. This laid him up for a long time and he could not work or renovate the properties. During that time interest rates increased and Mom became desperate.

It was around this time I dropped in for a cup of tea and she showed me what was going on. It was clear to me that she needed to sell all or most of the properties, and either live in the last remaining one or move north to a cheaper property.

Over the next three months, she sold all the houses and decided to move up north.

The house on Tannery Street was the last to be sold.

We discussed her options of finding a property up north where real estate was more reasonably priced.

During the sales negotiation of the Tannery home, she repeatedly asked the real estate agent if the buyer was the builder, or related to the builder, who planned to erect an apartment building directly behind her property.

Each time the real estate agent reassured her, "No." He said it was someone who wanted to tear down our home and build a bigger one on the property.

Mom agreed to the deal, but two days later she called me in a panic. "Tom, there were people here today banging stakes into the ground outside the house. I asked them who they were and they said they were with the builder who just bought our property."

The builder of the apartment building had in fact purchased Mom's house through a fraudulent offer; the real estate agent must disclose the purchaser of the property if asked. Mom was beside herself.

The next day I contacted the city planning office and found out the apartment complex owner was proposing to add further floors to the building, for which they needed more land coverage. A friend of mine worked in the office, so he pulled the permit application on this project, showing me the property drawings. I noticed many pencil marks on Mom's property.

This information confirmed the fraudulent offer.

Contacting the builder directly, I advised him that my mother was not going to honour the deal. If he wanted to renegotiate, he would deal with me. "No agents involved."

The night of the meeting I arrived at Mom's house an hour early. Mom had child-size chairs in her basement, used for her daycare business. They were between a kindergarten-sized and a normal chair. We put them in the living room on the other side of our coffee table.

I suggested that Mom, Steady Eddy, and I sit on the higher sectioned couch, positioning the builder, across from us in these preschool chairs. "This way they are forced to look up at us. Let's keep them uncomfortable in these tiny chairs," I told Mom. "When the builder looks at you, you look at *me*. That way he'll also look at me."

Of course, I did not want him to see that she was nervous, and I had to stop him from trying to intimidate her. At this stage of her life, she needed to take it easy and not be overstressed. She was anxious because this deal could help her get her next house. If it did not happen quickly, she feared losing it all.

Time was of the essence.

The builder was two hours late and came dressed in a big fur coat and Stetson hat. He drove a big black Cadillac. His drawings were under his arm. I directed him and his son to the living room daycare chairs. It was difficult to stop myself from laughing out loud, watching these robust men trying to get comfortable in these little chairs without breaking them.

The builder spread out his drawings over the coffee table and discussed his plans for a few minutes. We sat totally quiet and still. He looked at Mom three or four times and she looked at me.

Then I interrupted the builder, "We have no interest in what you're doing. Just put the drawings away. You've tried to take advantage of my family with a fraudulent offer. I'm preparing a letter to the local real estate board outlining the fraudulent activity associated with the offer. And I know the editor of the local *Mississauga News*, Ron Lennick. This issue will make a very interesting article, which could jeopardize the community's support of your project." I paused. "Please leave and return with a number. There will be no negotiating. This is a one-time offer, which we'll either accept or decline."

As he was leaving, he stopped at the door and said, "You'd better watch yourself if you contact the newspapers, young man."

"Are you threatening me?" I asked, but he opened the door and silently left, with his son in tow.

The next day I left for the Caribbean with my fiancée, Cathy. Mom called me three times that week in the hotel saying that the builder had not called back. I told her, "The man came to our house, and that means he wants the property. Stay patient, Mom."

Visiting Grandma's together

Upon my return, the builder called the next day to set up a second meeting. Out came the chairs from the basement again, and finally Mom got another 25% on top of the original sale price.

I am glad I could help her in this situation, protecting her the way she always looked after us and everyone else.

Mom used the proceeds from this sale to buy her next home north of Toronto, backing onto a farming property in Newton Robinson.

It was an old schoolhouse, and they divided the home into two residences. Our sister, Valerie, and her husband, Cam, with their sons, Danny and Tommy, lived on the right side, and Mom and "Steady Eddy" lived on the left side. They shared a big, beautiful entrance.

Lil's Angel

Another person whom Mom helped was her second husband's mother. His mother, Lil, came to live with Mom in her late sixties when she was failing. Mom set her up in the spare room and coached her through her death experience. Lil had been estranged from her son for many years. She had given up responsibility for him to her parents who raised him from four years old, while she went into the military. Now Lil was able to complete herself with her son, and with Mom's help, she dealt with her fear of death. Lil was so scared, that Margie could not leave her. She sat for hours holding her hand. Lil would shout for her when Mom left her side to use the bathroom. Our mother slept in the chair beside Lil's bed until the end.

Seeing and suffering so much heartbreak through her own life taught Mom to help anyone who needed her, whether it was family, friends, or acquaintances.

Mom did this naturally and with little decision process. Her positive influence, empathy, and compassion were her natural currency. If we, her children, ever challenged her on this decision, she always had the same response: "Hey, we will figure it out."

Chapter 9

Sowing

Orange Book

Mom believed we are all children of God—that we are the hands and fingers of God. But we have to make a conscious decision to use them.

Mom had an orange book with names of people in it and amounts of money she either gave them or loaned them. It was important for her to establish accountability and keep track.

Rick

When I was in grade 11, my friend, Rick, had a situation at home. Rick's mother and father had broken up and neither wanted to take the children. Seventeen-year-old Rick was the youngest of three kids. When Mom heard me speaking to my older sister in the kitchen, she poked her head in from the hallway and said, "Who are you talking about? Tom, go get that boy and put him in the spare bedroom."

Rick stayed with us on and off over the next three years. He had faced substance abuse and later found himself in a rehab centre in Buffalo, New York.

He's been clean ever since, is married and has a son.

He told me once, "Without your mother, none of this happens for me. I owe my life to her."

Sometimes our mother can be someone other than the one who birthed us.

From Rick

Spencer, my dear son, reminds me of Margie the most. Sometimes I look at him and think, "You have no idea, you would not exist. If not for Margie, I'd be in a ditch or dead."

The first time I walked through the double doors at 2nd Line West, even before I got in the hall, Margie Herstad landed me with a big hug and a peck too!

Since we were fifteen, Tom and I took the same school bus from Streetsville Secondary School. That's where we knew each other from, and became friends in wood-shop class and playing football together.

I remember that first day, Margie said, "We hug here!" I wasn't used to it. It felt awkward, but good at the same time.

Since then, she called me, "Soft Lips Hanlon." She taught me a family could laugh!

Tom had something I didn't even know existed. Everybody hugs each other! Basic affection. I wasn't accustomed to that. Where I came from, it was more like a verbal fight, every day! Affection only came when people were drunk, and they wanted to show off our sports trophies to company! Oh, we were the best then! When they were sober, oh no. Then we, the kids, went about our business and fended for ourselves.

I had a hard time accepting affection from anyone back then, still do.

(Julie, interviewing Rick, said to him, "What are you talking about? You give the best hugs ever!" Rick smiled.)

Sometimes I start off awkward inside, but I've gotten better over the years. With Margie, she didn't want anything from you! It felt different. As long as you were willing to work on yourself, she was all there for you.

She did kick me out once. She got tired of watching me go down, sleeping all the time, doing nothing, depressed, with no job. It hurt her to see me like that, day in, day out. It hurt to see me not making an effort for myself.

It was at the same door where I first met her that she told me I had to go. "You're not working on yourself, so you have to go." It killed her to say it. I could see it. Feel it.

During the following couple of years, I didn't keep in touch as much as I wanted; you know, you get doing your own thing, and life happens. But three years later, after finishing rehab down in Buffalo, I considered calling her. Margie would like to know I was doing better, and I wanted to talk to her.

She was thrilled and surprised to hear from me. "Where are you? What are you doing?" She asked. "Where are you going to go now?"

I said I didn't know. Hadn't gotten that far.

"Your room will be waiting for you when you get here!"

This actually took a load off me, as I hadn't fathomed where I would go next. I told her this. She was so proud that I came full circle, and back to her, this time to Tannery Street. The house was much smaller, but she always found room for someone.

You know, it's funny, at the beginning I always called her Mrs. Herstad. My parents, my Dad really, told us you never use an adult's first name! I remember once his friend Mike came over to our house and I said, "Hi, Mike!" and my father flew into the room, punched me in the head and yelled, "Don't ever do that. He's Mr. Jones to you!"

Yeah, that was my house.

But Margie wasn't having it. "Look, you have two choices," she told me. "Call me Mom or Margie, one of the two, but stop calling me Mrs. Herstad, okay? Just call me Mom!"

I had a hard time saying the word mom, so I called her Margie, but she was My Mom in every way.

She told me one night, "You don't have to be born to someone for them to be your mother! I am your mother. You were brought to me! I feel you are my son."

Wow. She always kept helping me change my life.

Back then, everybody got married, had kids, and did what was expected. It wasn't a choice or a conscious thing.

I believe that not everyone should have kids. So many people were victims to that culture. Didn't make them good parents, however.

So, I was meant to sit beside Tom in shop class!

I did have a page in the Orange Book, that tally of those who owed money they had borrowed from her or which she offered during life changes.

I had many entries in that book! At one time I was up to $5,000. But I would pay her here and there and brought it down to approximately $2,000.

When I came there from rehab, she knew I smoked. She didn't like it. But she would ask every day, "Do you need money for cigarettes?"

She'd give me $20 a day sometimes, and that added up. But she kept track in her Orange Book. She made people responsible for themselves.

A couple of years later, after I met and married my wife twenty-eight days after meeting her, Margie didn't flinch. I had been scared to tell her, but Margie simply flung her arms up for a hug, super thrilled for us.

Then, along came Spencer.

When he was born, Margie drove all the way down from Newton Robinson to Credit Valley to see him.

We took him up to see her, too. She took me around the corner to the Orange Book, and with a pen, marked in front of me, "PAID IN FULL!"

"Because you brought me that wonderful baby, and you have more important things to spend your money on, now." We hugged. Even if he doesn't remember her personally, Spencer knows today that he's here because of her!

Margie had insight like no one else. She told me I would meet and marry a girl with dark, curly hair! I did.

Margie's biggest impact on me is that she still helps me make the biggest decisions in my life, every day! She's always in my head.

Sometimes, I just talk to her.

I found it very difficult seeing her at the end, suffering, and I didn't go as often as I should have. But the last time I think was that day with Julie and Valerie. Margie saw me, even though she wasn't doing well. She looked up at me and puckered up for a kiss, and told me that she loved me! That was all she said, all she needed to say. Then a smile. I had to leave after that.

She knew it caused us pain to see her.

Whenever I get down too far, I always think of her.

She was my saviour. I would say, "Thank you for believing in me, for being there." She just took me in as if it was the most natural thing for her to do.

(In the interview, Julie reminded Rick that she saw his generous red rose arrangement at Margie's memorial night. The card read, "There would be no Rick, no Lori, and no Spencer, without you!")

I named my boat *Margie's Boyz*. This was Lori's idea, because all of us guys going north together were all connected to her. So it's perfect! Lori didn't know her that well, but she gets her! Lori knows that if Margie didn't rescue me, that she wouldn't have me or Spencer.

Spencer feels her by being around all of you Herstad's. He reminds me of Margie the most.

Affection is a learned behaviour. It's more natural now in our household to hug and kiss my son hello or goodnight, even at age eighteen. Margie would bawl and be thrilled to know that. She brings it out in us both. She triggered it in Spencer because she's still around him.

I would be worse to people if I didn't know her! I mean, I'm not fond of people in general. When I'm in the truck, I have no stereo on. I just sit quietly.

At some point each day, invariably, she comes into my mind.

She says, "Gently!", "Don't get your nose outa' joint!" to help me stop the anger that can rise within me.

One great memory was the night I worked New Year's Eve, in the restaurant business.

This was before Lori. I was alone, living in the little white cottage on the other side of the pool on the Herstad property. On the porch, I saw that the light was on. The door flung open and Margie came towards me with her arms outstretched, and said, "Ricky, get in here!" She landed a hug and we talked for two hours.

She knew I was trying to stay sober. I was working.

(Julie adds in the interview, "You know she was waiting for you! She knew you'd be alone, maybe a little sad not to have plans or a special someone, so she waited up for you to come home, to love on you.") I know Margie changed my life. I cried in front of her. I still get pissed that she's not here. But her lesson to me was not to sit and stew in it. Get up, don't think of yourself, go to another meeting, or go help a friend.

She'd say, "I believe…" never, "You should…" I love her!

Our Nicknames

Her nickname for me was "Sugar Fella Boo." One of my favourite childhood experiences was Mom's famous back scratches. I remember running to her, sitting on the couch, pulling up my shirt and laying across her lap asking her for "scratch-back." She would scratch with her long finger-nails as long as I wanted while softly saying, "Sugar Fella Boo, I love you. Sugar Fella Boo, I love you."

Julie's nickname was "Sugar Girl."

Mom called my son, her "Golden Boy." Reigan is a mixed child, as I am white and his mother, Cathy, is from Port of Spain, Trinidad.

Reigan (age 4) and I at Steve's Wedding

Mom did not want Reigan to wonder where he belonged and wanted him to own his unique identity.

She sat him down one day in the kitchen when she lived with me. He was three, and she said to him, "Reigan, you're the colour we will all be one day. You represent the colour we will be when all people, from extreme black to extreme white and all the colours in between, meet in the middle. You're ahead of your time. You're the colour that people go to tanning salons to look like."

Nature Hour

When we had babies under two visiting us on hot summer days, Mom stripped the kids down and let them run around outside. She would also take them into the pool for a frolicking, fun time.

The excitement on these little ones' faces, running, laughing, and swimming in the nude was a joy to witness.

"Loving Them Through It All of it"

This was Mom's answer when we would ask about people she was helping. Whenever we asked Mom how she would handle a problem, or if any of us had a difference of opinion with anyone, she would say one word: "Gently." I remember this word was one she would say to you with her eyes first. But if you did not get it, she would say it out loud.

Just like Rick remembers fondly.

Man in the Mirror

Mom said, "There's far too much emphasis on Jesus. He was the messenger. The emphasis should be on his message. When religion expresses to you to give your life to Jesus, I believe it's the Jesus in each of us we should give ourselves to, instead of the separate Jesus who lived."

This particular saying of Mom's reminds me of a most moving experience I had. It occurred when I was twenty-five. It was during a move. I passed a full-length mirror in the living room and saw myself in my peripheral vision. I stopped and turned to face myself.

I became fixed on looking into my own eyes.

I was drawn in with such a strong curiosity and desire to see something in myself. As I gazed into my eyes, the mirror image of my body faded away and all I saw was my upper chest, neck, face, and head. The image drew me in closer and even closer still.

Then my face morphed into the face of Jesus and I saw his crown of thorns, his beard.

Moved to tears, the energy of this experience overwhelmed me so much, I had to turn away.

I broke down with emotion. Just as I was collecting myself, the phone rang. It was my mother, with whom I was sharing the other part of the house. She had picked up on the energy on her side of the house and asked what happened.

When I told her, she said, "God was making you aware of the Christ that is inside you and he was showing you that you are a direct child of God." She added, "We're all children of God. It's about being consciously aware of this fact that makes all the difference in this world. Because it relates to how we treat one another and how we respond to each other."

Mom believed that all religions were equal; all working to understand the same source, which she defined as God, Our Father, or Our Lord or The Higher Power, The Source.

Mom's Second Marriage

I could say much about Mom's second marriage, but from my perspective, I saw it as a three-part issue. I believe it must have been very difficult for her second husband to live under the shadow of my father, knowing that my Dad was her first and only love. The second part being that we kids were all very strong personalities who could be much to handle at times. The deal breaker occurred when he sided against Mom with another member of our family.

From Mom's perspective, this was a point of no return.

As expressed earlier, Mom remarried in 1992 and they moved up north to Newton Robinson. They shared the old schoolhouse, which had been divided into two homes, with Valerie, her husband, and their two boys, Danny and Tommy.

When families live together, misunderstandings can sometimes bring friction into the home. After one such argument, Mom's husband refused to speak with my sister Valerie and her husband for almost a year.

Valerie told me, "He had misunderstood my words during our disagreement, believing that I'd said that all the assets belonged to Dad and Mom. Offended, he felt I was disrespecting him. He shunned me from then on."

This weighed heavily on Mom, and whenever I visited, the tension in the house was obvious.

Because of the silence between them, a major unresolved issue could not be addressed without dialogue. Valerie and Cam wanted to sell the house and move on, but Mom's second husband refused to discuss the subject of selling. Mom did not know how to deal with this situation, and as a result, became depressed and started over-medicating herself with prescription drugs. She would often retreat and lie in the dark seclusion of her room on the top level of the house. It was obvious to me that something had to change.

After being diagnosed with Parkinson's disease, Mom's health was deteriorating, with her energy nowhere like it had been before.

All this came to a head in 1997 when Mom was taken to hospital in Newmarket. Stressed and upset, Valerie told me, "I cannot do this anymore. Take care of Mom. This is costing me my marriage."

"I'll take care of Mom," I said. "Get back to focusing on your marriage." Valerie was always a caregiver, always there at the drop of a hat, the nurturer in our family. I realized that Valerie was exhausted and consumed by looking after Mom. On top of the depression and suffering with Parkinson's disease, Mom was also dealing with a host of health issues, including a bladder infection that would not go away.

Valerie thanked me for helping.

After divorcing her second husband, and briefly staying up north in Midland on Georgian Bay with a friend, Mom then moved in with Reigan and me in Mississauga.

Before Mom moved in, I sat my son down and asked him for his help. "Grandma's going to stay with us for a while, so that means we need to make room for her. Other than my room and the office, there's your room. Would you be okay with giving Grandma your room?"

Reigan looked at me with big eyes and asked, "Where do I sleep?"

"You'd have to sleep with me, but it'll only be until we figure everything out. Are you okay with letting Grandma sleep in your room for a while?"

"You bet, Dad," he said before I finished the sentence. He was still young enough to enjoy sleepovers with Dad.

"Would you go to Grandma and offer her your room?"

It was adorable watching him respond to me and then seeing him deliver his message of support to his Grandmother.

Living with us, her depression soon lifted. She read all day, the Bible, and a book about Nostradamus. She researched books about angels, and accepted a board position with the local Parkinson's Association. She was an active member with the association from 1999 to 2005. I took her to a local church twice a week for her to be included in seniors stitching and meditation class.

Again, I saw Mom in action, admiring her strong and exquisite spiritual awareness and her influence on this world. Even in her frail state, she continued to reinforce the need in us to help one another.

I remember once seeing Mom in my living room, crying tears of joy, watching *The Oprah Winfrey Show*, as Whitney Houston and Mariah Carey sang, "When You Believe."

At around the time Mom moved in with us, I was going through my own marriage breakup, and this allowed us to help each other.

As I was also starting up my new business and Reigan was still a preschooler, Mom was quick to pitch in.

Reigan was with me Tuesdays, Wednesdays, and every other weekend. But as my ex-wife's schedule was busy as a makeup artist for film and television, I had him more often. I told her that Reigan could come any time and could stay longer. Knowing that they grow up quickly and (as they say) in the blink of an eye, his childhood would be gone, I took any and all opportunities to be with him. I wanted to be part of his life. All of it.

This was when Mom offered me the best advice I could have received.

Through the process of my marriage breaking up and the separation, Cathy and I had many disagreements. One evening at the kitchen table, Mom said to me, "When you pick up Reigan or drop him off to Cathy, as you respond to her, I want you to see your son's face in front of hers. Because you're teaching him how to talk to women. You're also teaching him to respect his mother. If she says something that upsets you, tell her you'll call her later to discuss it, and then leave."

Yet another one of the greatest gifts, Mom gave me.

I Am Ready

After my marriage ended, I was without anyone in my life for fourteen months. When I returned to my house from my first date with

Jules, the lady I am with today, I passed Mom in my open-concept living area. She reclined in her favourite front-window love-seat. Although Mom was living with me, she did not know I was seeing anyone. But as I walked into the kitchen, I heard her say, "You have met someone," in a soft whisper.

Mom had picked up on my energy, feeling the subtle difference in me. She could still read people around her, especially us, her loved ones.

I said, "Yes, I have."

Mom said, "It's the lovely blonde girl Chris told me about." Chris was Mom's psychic friend, whom she had asked about me shortly after my marriage breakup. Now Mom remembered when Chris had said that I would meet a blonde woman to whom I would give my heart.

These were special times; those spent living together with my mother in her later years. We reunited during this time, enjoying our chance to bond again on a different level.

Over time, it became obvious that Mom needed her independence, and we each needed our living space back. I had a tenant leave my basement apartment and Mom moved in, settling in quite nicely. She was still close so we could continue helping each other in our transitions.

Later, when my younger sister Julie's marriage ended, she returned from California and joined Mom in the basement apartment. Julie had to regroup in her life and being close to Mom was imperative.

Julie later bought a beautiful end unit townhouse backing onto a forest. Mom moved in with her to be together. It was a wonderful time for them and they were also close to us. When this arrangement ran its course, Mom moved into the cottage at the back of our old property on Tannery.

It so happened that a friend was renting our old home on Tannery from that builder.

The cottage at the back of the property that Mom had created years earlier was now available to her. With other people's help, we got that place spruced up for her. She loved being back by the babbling brook with the weeping willow trees towering over the cottage.

It was also just a walk across the field to my home.

From the cottage, Mom eventually moved into a participation housing program after a one-year waiting period. Mom had realized while keeping her independence, she did need some assistance at times, and this in-the-building staff-assistance program was perfect. It was a five-minute drive to Aghabi Place, in Mississauga, so she was still close by. *Aghabi* in Turkish means a title of respect, often used with the title of a senior position.

It was very important to Mom to be financially independent, and this program was perfect as it was adjusted to meet her individual financial capacity. Mom remained here and forged wonderful relationships with the staff.

Reigan and I stopped in all the time. We enjoyed dinners together and trips to the store. During this time, Mom began needing a walker and we got her a good one. If she did not want to wait for us to take her shopping, she could now make it happen on her own. The grocery store was very close, directly behind her building.

Her stay at Aghabi Place ended when I got several calls from the participation staff expressing Mom's decline. She was experiencing hallucinations caused by taking medication for Parkinson's over a long period. She also had challenges remembering her medication schedule, and the staff could not take responsibility for this part of her care.

To help me understand the new situation, Donna, a lovely, older lady on staff, suggested I spend a night with Mom, to get some perspective. I agreed, and during that night, Mom woke me twice from my makeshift bed on the living room floor telling me that something had to be done to control the young children who were coming out of the cabinet below the kitchen sink.

It was obvious that we needed to look for a 24/7 care facility for her. At a joint meeting to address Mom's move from this building and into a nursing home, I remember the staff were highly emotional. One even cried as we discussed the details involved in this move, and the necessary documents to be completed. They were losing someone they cared for deeply.

My girlfriend Jules and I went looking for nursing homes to ensure we made the best choice for Mom. After visiting five or six facilities, we narrowed it down to two. We took Mom to both places so she could make the final decision for herself.

This was an interesting process for me. In addition to the sales pitch, what it boiled down to was the vibe in the lunchroom or dining room. When I saw all the staff and residents together, it gave me the best read on a facility.

Mom's choice was the Grace Manor building in Holland Christian Homes. Here, her medication was managed, and she had constant nursing staff around her. Mom participated in many programs and her favourite was music night on Thursday evenings. Local musicians came in to perform.

Fortunately for me, Grace Manor was across the street from my Thursday night hockey games, and I participated with her before my game, holding hands together and listening to the music.

We visited Mom often, taking her out of her room if she was there, settling in the lounge to talk. Other times we had dinner at the restaurant on the ground floor in the east wing.

We also took her out for her favourite spaghetti dinner, which was fifteen minutes away in North Brampton. Another one of our, fun excursions, was taking her for a chocolate-dipped Dairy Queen ice cream. In warm weather, we often went for a drive to get her out, with windows down and the music turned up as high as she wanted.

As always, music was such an integral part of Mom's life. In addition to continuing to share soulful, emotive songs between Julie and myself over the years, one of the pure joys I experienced was when I was driving Mom on a country road heading to Terra Cotta. It was just me and Mom and Whitney Houston on the radio, singing, "I Love the Lord."

The sky was clear blue and the wind rushed through the open car windows. We were riding down a big hill and over a bridge with little cottages clustered along the riverbank. The song started very slow, then ramped up, and when the chorus kicked in, it sounded like a freight train blaring in the song. Mom and I were holding hands and she shook with excitement as she heard this chorus engage. Feeling her reaction, I also got chills. It was another moment we shared, one when I felt more alive than ever before.

I visited Mom on my own or with Reigan at least once a week. One day I called her and asked for a dinner date, saying that I would pick her up at five o'clock.

Often, I was late, and this time I was at least thirty minutes late. I called to have her not be included in the facility dinner, and she waited patiently for me in her room.

I came in and was in a rush. I was quick with the hello, grabbed her wheelchair from the other end of her room, got her into the chair, and headed out with her.

At one point, I realized I had not signed her out, so I left her in the hallway, and went back to the desk for a moment.

When I finally pushed her into the elevator, the door closed and it was just the two of us.

Mom said, "You're very good at your duty."

Her words hit me hard. I gasped, realizing I was often in such a rush that I was not present with her. I was in "get it done" mode.

Sometimes I was so caught up in my head and busy with my thoughts that I did not see her, have her see me listening to her, and let her witness my facial expressions change when she said something that stirred me or my imagination.

These are the times I have wasted. These are the times I wish I could do over. I would say to my mother, "I'm so sorry for those times I was in a rush and I made you feel you were my duty and not my choice." And she would probably smile.

Mom got along with everyone, but she told me she did not feel completely comfortable around one female caregiver at Grace Manor.

"Everyone here is wonderful except this one nurse," Mom whispered, pointing her out to me. She was tall and had masculine-looking facial features.

One evening I went in to see Mom and this same lady pulled me aside. She said, "I was away on vacation for a week. When I got back, the first time I walked into your Mothers's room, I walked past her bed to put her washed clothes in her cabinet. I had my back to her, and I didn't even notice if she saw me come in. I heard her say, 'I missed you,' in her soft voice." She paused, and with tears in her eyes, added, "Mr. Herstad, hearing your mother say that to me meant so much."

Mom had touched another soul. Even as her body declined, and she was increasingly losing her independence, becoming more reliant on others, from her prone position, she could still touch another with her words, with her love.

Thirtieth Celebration

For Mom's Thirty-Year AA Birthday at her Streetsville group, I planned to meet my family at the location. Julie and Valerie were going to bring Mom over. But Valerie called me from Holland Christian Homes and said that her Parkinson's had kicked in bad that night. She was in no shape to go to her honorary meeting. When I spoke to Mom on the phone, telling her that I would accept this recognition on her behalf, I asked what she wanted me to say to the members.

"Please tell them to *keep coming back*," she said. I addressed the fellowship with my own words prior to delivering Mom's message. I shared with them how Mom had found AA and how her membership had brought our mother back to us and saved her life all those years ago. I described how she knew she was in the right place from the first time she came through the doors of AA. God bless you, Bill W.

Our Evolving Relationship

My relationship with my mother went through many changes as it evolved. She gave me life. She protected me. She fed me. She watched out for me. She always thought about me. She provided for me. She always had time for me. She got excited for me. She warned me of certain people and of choices I might make.

She always saw the best in me.

As the years passed, our roles shifted. This happened gradually. It was now my turn to look out for Mom, to take care of her, to provide for her, and yes, to feed her. It was now my duty and desire to do for her, to remind her of who she was. I always thought about her. I have always thought about my mother my whole life, but at this stage it was different. This big shift helped me realize and appreciate even more, from a new perspective, how much she did for me.

Now our roles were reversed. I never asked her to explain herself. I gave my opinion only when asked. It was important to show her ongoing respect to allow her continued dignity. I think that if we do not do this for our parents, they can keep secrets from us and find freedom from us in other relationships.

Mom did not need to be drinking an alcoholic beverage to make a toast with her glass. Her toast was as follows:

She would place her glass above yours and say, "Never above you." She would place her glass below yours and say, "Never below you."

Then she would place her glass beside yours and say, "Always right by your side."

Journey Over

Late in July of 2011, Mom was moved from Grace Manor in Brampton to the hospital via ambulance. The nursing staff advised me that she was failing quickly, and I rushed to the hospital to meet the ambulance there.

When I got to the hospital, Julie had already arrived. They had Mom stationed in a hallway, since there was a backlog for beds. We spent much of that night waiting with her in that congested hallway.

At one point, Julie lost it with the staff. It was an anxious time for us all, and things can boil over when you are holding onto patience with your fingertips. It was close to 3 am before they got our mother into a room.

The following day we stayed with Mom together, as well as in shifts, so there was always someone with her. When Julie and Valerie went to the store for something, I had a chance to sit with my mom alone and hold her hand for most of that afternoon.

She was unconscious, but stable.

At one point she rose from the bed to a straight-backed seated position, her eyes opened wide. I was witnessing her death experience. I had discussed this with her at times in the past about her facilitating others with their death. Years ago, she had told me, "They witness either someone from their past who was deceased, an angel, or a presentation of a Jesus entity as they interpret him. Whichever one they see, the message is the same: I'm here to guide you home."

As I write this, I wonder how she knew that. I wish I had asked her that. As she sat up, I whispered to her, "Who do you see, Mom? Who is there?"

She did not answer. After about a count of five, she lay back down and was unconscious again.

Later that night she made a remarkable, complete recovery. We were totally amazed.

We had wonderful conversations with her, and she was clear minded and well spoken. I could not believe the change in her. On the way home that night around 11:30 pm, I called her sister in Niagara Falls to relay the fantastic news.

Little did I know or realize this was her last amount of energy that she could muster for a final interaction with her children.

Exhausted and relieved at my mother's obvious recovery, I slept until 10:30 the next morning. I was ready to head to the hospital when the phone rang. It was Valerie. I could hear my other sister, Julie, weeping in the background. She told me that the hospital just called her.

Mom was gone.

All that could come out of my mouth was, "No. No. No."

After pausing for what seemed like eons, I told Valerie I would meet them in Mom's hospital room. On my way to the hospital, I got pulled over by the police. Immediately, I got out of my vehicle, rushed to the police car, and told the constable that my mother had just passed, and I was desperately trying to get to the hospital to see her and meet my sisters. Walking me back to my car, the policeman tried his best to calm me down and then let me continue without a ticket, as long as I agreed to watch my speed.

In the hospital room, Valerie and Julie sat beside Mom's bed. Julie was a mess and Valerie rose to embrace me. We hugged and moved arm in arm to Mom's bedside.

Valerie whispered in my ear, "She's still warm. Does that mean her spirit is still in the room?"

Mom looked so peaceful and rested now. Her suffering was over. She had released herself with no struggle, her doctor told us. Then she said that she had been taking Mom's blood pressure when Mom went. "I've never experienced a death with such ease before. I could feel your mother's love go through me as she passed. I'll never forget the feeling I experienced."

Mom had touched another even in her death. Julie had brought some music to play for our mother, and the three of us sat in her room for another hour with our mother and the music around us.

It was during this time that we came completely together again. We addressed any past issues, and they were all resolved. It was obvious to us all, the time we had wasted bickering and arguing at times.

This often happens in a family with strong type-A personalities, when during family crises, each tries to force their will on the others. Diplomacy is the working operative, and in many cases, I knew that my delivery was far from good. Why was I trying to be so strong, all the time?

Now, listening to the music, my two sisters and I told each other what we had to say about the past, apologizing for each of our own parts in any disputes.

The three of us cried and held each other.

We looked at Mom, now deceased in that bed, and I heard her in my head say, "The body is a bag of bones and when we pass on, the spirit goes home, because our spirit is everlasting and just changes form."

This gave me a bit of comfort as I stood there staring at my mother. At one point, Julie rushed to the bathroom to vomit, as her grief overwhelmed her.

We three left that room together with our arms around each other, walking the hallway to the elevator. I have always wished our oldest sister, Cynthia, could have shared that experience with us. Cynthia had come and said her goodbyes the day before.

Kissing her on the forehead, the last thing I said to my mother before I left the room, "Sugar Fella Boo loves you."

My grief when dealing with Mom's passing came as waves washing over my body that literally kept robbing my breath. I had to fight to regulate it, to continue breathing. It would take me many long months to find myself again.

The service was held at a beautiful funeral home in Oakville, Ontario, thanks to my common-law wife, Jules, who knows how to make the right decisions in times of confusion. Once again, Jules saved me from myself.

After collecting my thoughts and writing Mom's eulogy, Jules asked me if I was ready for the service.

I nodded, "I think so, yes."

"No, you're not, Tom. Do it for me three times." We sat at the kitchen table, and I went through it with her.

I did not experience the torturing grief writing the eulogy, but when I expressed it in spoken words to Jules, I was over-whelmed, could not get through it without breaking a few times. It was brutal, but after the third reading, I was ready. My Jules had prepared me.

The last thing I had to do was to visit the funeral home and familiarize myself with the room. I did this the following day.

The day of the service was a beautiful summer blue-sky day. Before we entered the chapel, Lee, our half-sister—Mom's gift to another mother—arrived. I had sent the service information to her home near Ottawa. She came directly in front of me and looked at me as if she had finally found someone in a crowd. We fixed on each other's eyes and I remember wondering, for a split second, who she was. I was still in a fog and desperately trying to process information through the continuing shock of losing my mother.

The second I realized it was Lee, I grabbed her and we embraced. She sat directly behind the immediate family after being given the option to sit with us or in the second pew.

Julie joined Lee and held her hand.

There was a delay in some of our family members getting to the service, so I announced we were going to wait for them.

Over the next fifteen minutes, something interesting happened. While waiting, the entire congregation started establishing a sense of community. People turned around in their seats to talk to each other and began sharing stories in little groups.

As I observed this connectivity, instead of the wait making things awkward, it occurred to me that Mom would have loved the interaction happening.

It was becoming a celebration.

Once the rest of the clan arrived, everyone was present, the service commenced. During Mom's service, two of her grandsons, Dylan and Gavin Moore, each played the guitar and sang a song for their grandmother. Other than witnessing the birth of my son, these were the proudest moments of my life.

I shared some of the stories you have just read. Halfway through the eulogy, the room changed. As I was speaking, I felt my mother's love come into the room. This sensation overwhelmed me and I stopped, looked around, and stammered. Turning away from the podium where I stood, I looked behind me. I tried to catch my breath.

From halfway back in the crowd, Rick picked up on what was happening and yelled out, "Love you, Tom!"

Hearing his words, I snapped back, found my composure again, and faced the congregation. I leaned into the microphone and said, "Love you too, Rick."

I was back on course. Afterwards, I thanked him for saving me.

My last statement of Mom's eulogy was, "Now, I know what happened as she approached the Pearly Gates; God said, 'Stand back and open the gates wide. Here she comes!' And in a thundering voice He added, *'Well done, my dear! Well done!'*"

Everyone was deeply moved by the entire service. It was due to the sum of many things: the minister's clear expression of Mom's caring ways; the impact of Mom's two grandsons singing for her on this day; the impact of the eulogy; and the people's emotions during the memorial video and selected music Julie had chosen. Throughout Mom's life, music always played an important part. She turned to it for entertainment, inspiration, escape, and in times of change. On this day of her celebration, it was very much present.

The last video picture was a shot of Mom and Dad in a boat together, heading for open waters, happy and in their twenties.

The service truly was a family effort. The effect was obvious when many in attendance who had not known Mom expressed, "I feel like I met your mother today."

Then we went to the reception together to celebrate Mom's life.

Here is an email my sister asked be included in this book. It is to her fellow workers at her corporate office before the service took place.

From Julie:

My mother passed away very peacefully Friday morning, finally ending a very difficult chapter in our family's lives, in the most gentle and serene way.

I met the ambulance as they arrived at her nursing home, late afternoon Wed. I was able to be inside the ambulance to comfort her, hold her hand, and be by her side. She was found unresponsive, similar to what occurred last December, almost indiscernible blood pressure.

They were able to stabilize her but it was apparent that she was in multiple organ failure by her initial blood tests as well as dealing with another infection similar to in Dec.

Each of my 3 siblings and I, as well as many 30+yr friends of hers and childhood mates of ours gathered for us and were able to say their own goodbyes and thank you's to my mother. It was magical. I myself had a very good long talk with her. Although she was in a semi-comatose state, she would acknowledge by a squeeze of the hand or by pursing her lips for a kiss. I asked the universe if I might be granted one more gift before they answered my long-time prayer of ending her state of limbo these last 18 months, by having her perk up enough to look at each of us with those beautiful baby blues, and I said, "Your work here is done, love. Go fly free and dance with our father again." The next morning she departed the body. The doctor met with all of us afterward and informed us that in her career, she has never felt such a presence and witnessed her passing with such grace that it moved her. And p.s. Her Friday 9 am blood work came back with normal levels. There was no more infection. They don't understand this. I do. Our prayers were answered that she had our full blessing to go. Our only wish was there would be no struggle, no pain. What a beautiful gift.

Please let all know I am ok. Just will require a few days.

Service is being held tomorrow, Tues. evening @ 7 pm at Glen Oaks, 3146 Ninth Line, Oakville.

Donations may be made in our mother's name, Mary Margaret Herstad, to the Parkinson's Foundation of Canada.

As you have experienced throughout this read, poetry has been much a part of my family. I share with you a poem I wrote for my mother the day of her passing:

My Mother

You brought me into this world

You gave me life

You fed me

You held me

You comforted me

You protected me

You showed the truth to me

You showed me the way

About you, there is so much to say

You taught love, care, and share

The lives you touched

The listening you did

The love you gave

I hold you in my heart

Until my end, right from the start

I know when I am finished my time

Seeing you again will be my sign

And on that day

There will be again so much to say.

Mom believed in reincarnation and that we have been here many times before, and the reason for our return is the lessons we have yet to learn here on Earth, serving to advance our consciousness.

Two days after Mom's service, I stood waiting for the coffee to brew, looking out the kitchen window into the backyard. I noticed two white butterflies. They flew in circles together within the confines of the window frame. They seemed to dance like moving poetry. I watched them for about thirty seconds, spellbound. Then one left the frame of the window but the other stayed for another few seconds, and then flew away.

I strained to watch the butterfly flutter through my backyard. It met the other butterfly that seemed to wait on the top of the fence. Then they both flew towards the neighbour's yard and out of sight.

I was positive these were my parents, saying, "We're together again," and as it happened in life, Dad left early and then Mom left to join him.

If I had not completely understood her message, Mom made sure I did not doubt that this was another "Godincidence," part of her back-up plan.

When I logged onto the computer later that morning, Chris, one of Mom's best friends, sent me a Facebook picture of a butterfly in her garden. The caption said, "Your Mom asked me to send you this picture." Chris is a psychic. This picture was of a copper butterfly garden ornament that Mom had given her to enjoy in her garden.

Lee

A few months after Mom's passing, I invited Lee over for dinner and she graciously made the long trip to my home. She travelled through this way to get to Port Colborne where she grew up and still has many friends.

On this wonderful visit, I cooked for her for the first time.

We had not yet had a chance to be alone, just the two of us. Our conversations helped me truly feel and understand Lee's emotional journey through contacting the adoption agency, and starting the reunion process with her birth mother, our mother. She shared with me her binder with all the legal correspondence with the agency, and every letter Mom had ever written to her.

We also discussed her children and her husband's death. Lee told me about her husband's heart attack on the beach during a vacation in the Caribbean, and how she got him home. She shared her loving thoughts on their entire relationship, and when she was finished, I felt as though I began to know him. How proud she was of her children, and how excited she was to be a grandmother.

I easily saw in her the kindness and strength I had witnessed throughout the years in our mother.

Then Lee told me something that blew me away, I asked her, "If Mom was here right now, what would you say to her?"

"Tom, I speak to her all the time. Just the way I'm speaking to you now," she told me. "And how I loved the conversations with Margie about UFOs!"

Not only did Mom give such a wonderful gift to Lee's adoptive parents all those years ago, but Lee continues to be a gift in our lives.

Nana's Gift

One other thing that Mom's death righted, despite past family tensions, was when, as a sign of respect, my father's mother, our Nana, Mildred Herstad, honoured Mom's life by paying for her funeral and getting her a plot with the family, so, "Margie could be buried with her husband and near other family members."

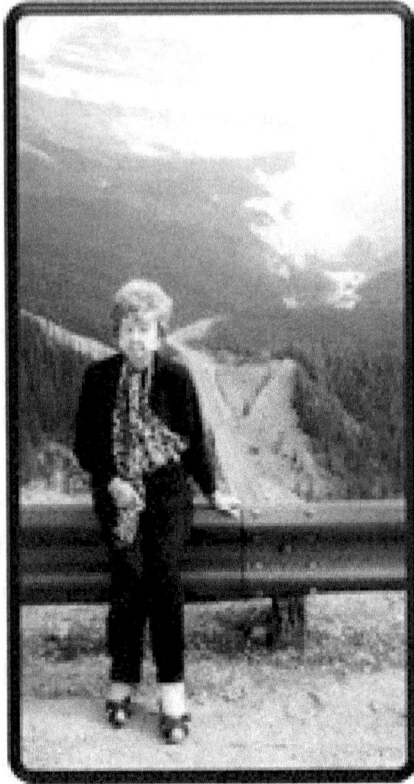

Nana, Mildred Herstad, age 96, Jasper, Alberta

Mom was buried with our father on his birthday, September 3rd, 2011. After a prayer and a personal poem specially selected by my oldest sister, Cynthia, and recited by my brother-in-law, David Moore, I knelt down with the green, rectangular urn and rested it into the ground on top of our father's grave.

They were together again.

I believe that Mom had never felt completely accepted by our Nana because of her teenage pregnancy. Now I felt that this magnanimous gesture was deeply healing on many levels. God Bless you, Mildred.

Nana passed away in 2014 at 102.

Cathy

Going through the hard time of divorce for me and my son, and trying to move on with my life, I never realized the impact of my mother's love and influence on my ex-wife, Cathy. Yet again, I recognized how writing this book has helped me heal and further understand those around me.

When interviewing my ex-wife, I witnessed something I never noticed while we were together. The way Cathy expressed her admiration and love for Mom was surprising, and yet so beautiful.

After remembering fun times they had shared together, Cathy's jovial laughter slowly died down. Cathy turned pensive, as if searching for the most fitting words to honour Margie, the mother-in-law she loved tremendously.

I had not known this.

While we were together, I only remember a mutual respect Mom and Cathy had for one another. I never knew the depth of their bond, until now.

As Cathy spoke, her voice got softer, and deep emotion was all over her face. "Margie had such a presence. I am so grateful that her blood and her essence have passed down to my son, that she's part of us, our family, and always will be. I feel nothing but gratitude to be part of her life, to be loved by her. When I met Margie, the first thing she said was that I was a gift from God to her son. What acknowledgment! And she made me feel special." Tears rolled down Cathy's cheeks as she added softly, "When I was with her, Margie *always* made me feel very special. She made me feel worthy. If you didn't know her, you'd still feel that no matter what, she would impact your life with a level of understanding, kindness, and love—that she'd inspire you, elevate you."

She sighed, "I miss her a lot. She was also my friend. I could tell her anything, even more than I could tell my own mother, or you, Tom. When I think of her, I'm reminded to give people a few minutes of my time, to make eye contact, and to be present with them. Margie would never tell you what to do or what to feel. She listened without judgment, letting you be yourself with total acceptance, letting you feel that you would make the right decision, whatever the obstacle. She was a beautiful spirit. No matter what she went through, she remained untainted, just full of love, regardless of her own hardships."

Jules

From the very first moment I met Jules in 1998, I had the exact same reaction as my father did when he first saw my mother at the dance.

In a room full of people, I only saw Jules.

She fills me with joy, peace, and a sense of calm. I think about her all the time. When I see something on my own, I get excited, anticipating sharing it with Jules, and her reaction to it. Often, hearing music, especially when driving through the countryside with the windows down, has inspired me to write poems for her.

The generous soul that Jules is, she's been patient with me throughout the hard times, and we have gotten to know each other and have committed to each other over the years.

As my mother taught us to remember, none of us is perfect and each of us is a constant work in progress.

My son means everything to me. He is my legacy, but Jules is the light and love of my life.

During many grief-filled months after Mom's passing, I needed to centre myself. I withdrew, sold my home, and moved into my trailer. The pressure on my relationship with Jules during this time was difficult for us both. In my hermit stage of life, I was like a lobster that had outgrown his shell, hiding under a rock to shed and grow a bigger and stronger shell.

When I was ready, I came out of my hiding place to carry on with my journey.

I continued taking walks along the river, listening to the birds, watching the sunrise and sunset over the fields, starting to cook for whomever came over. All the while, I continued searching deeply within myself, listening to the inner voice.

I decided to travel in the trailer with my son, Reigan. My sister, Julie, came for the first half of the trip. The thirty-one-day tour also took us through St. Louis to see my cousin Barbie and her family.

Then we travelled through the Grand Canyon, Sedona, a gorgeous place north of Santa Monica (where Reigan turned twenty), San Diego, Houston, Galveston, New Orleans, and we finished in Nashville.

During this trip I constantly listened to satellite radio, channel 128, to Joel Osteen, an inspired Christian man. For many hours, I listened to his uplifting messages of possibility and positivity. I even went to his ministry to attend his service in Lakewood, and met the man. This was another checkmark on my bucket list.

Recently, my sister, Julie, reminded me about my incredible reaction and personal experience at the Grand Canyon. In 1998, Julie had taken Mom to see the Grand Canyon. She told me that my reaction upon seeing the gigantic, ancient, red and gold shapes carved out of Mother Nature's land was identical to Mom's spiritual connection all those years ago.

Julie said to me, "Because of Mom, we feel these things at a transcendental level, not just as a viewer. We drink it in and it becomes part of our spirit because of her influence on us, and because we are part of her DNA."

That day, over my two-hour walk around the Grand Canyon, I felt as insignificant as a grain of sand on a shore, and yet completely in sync with the universe as a spiritual being having a human experience. At one point, I found myself standing, gazing over the Grand Canyon. I remembered this was the very place where my mother had stood and marvelled at the magic of this awesome view. I recognized the spot from a picture of Mom and Julie on their visit here.

I was never the same after this experience.

Upon my return home, I found the perfect place to live, in the country. It is a unique 1922 farmhouse on a large property with six alpacas, two miniature horses, two goats, two sheep, hens, a rooster, geese galore, a bald eagle, and a horse named Duke.

I call this place Shangri-La. This was where I was inspired to start writing. And to find my way back to Jules.

Over the years since I have known this lady, I realize that my father's poem to my mother, from all those years ago, captures my gratitude for our own relationship.

We're stronger than ever, as partners in life. As we are all on a constant journey of self-discovery and learning, I know that as long as we are together, I am rowing with passion, and the water is calm and the sky is blue as far as the eye can see.

When things feel right in this life, even if you deny them, they never go away.

From Jules

"There are some people we meet in life whose energy seems to sparkle around them. These people are human angels who have learned to let go of the patterns of life and embrace all that is good." —Steven Aitchison

The above is one of my favourite quotations. And I describe Margie as an Earth Angel. Margie impacted everyone she touched. She always made me feel loved. When I think of her, my heart swells, and it always will. I know she loved me.

Margie used to say, "Tommy could be a bully, you know?" And she would tell him, "Gently!"

Margie's Hugs! When I first met her, I felt her so full of love and kindness, and joy and hope too! She embraced all my staff at the gym; she went over to every one of them and had to hug them!

I don't think I have met anyone like her. The warmth! Her unstoppable heart! Even if someone hurt her or took from her, she would never stop loving them. She would still take them back.

She was forgiveness, at its best.

You always left with a piece of her with you. Margie was and is Unconditional Love.

If I struggle about Tom, I think of her and I instantly feel calm, that everything will be okay.

A psychic once told me, "Mary Margaret is here!" So I know she is with me if I need her.

She showed us you can "be" Love, but be strong, too. She managed to ignite a father presence for Tom, too, and managed to bring out his softness.

I think of her love for her husband, the father of her loving children, and the music.

Every time I hear Vikki Carr sing, "It Must Be Him," of course, I think of her.

If I had a chance to tell her one last thing, it would be, "Thank you for bringing so much love into my life and for making me feel so special. I love you and I want to be like you!"

Chris was one of my mother's closest friends for over 40 years. They shared many very interesting conversations because Chris is a psychic. Chris has been cited in earlier pages. When asked to participate in this project, the following was her tribute to her special friend Margie.

From Chris Price

I will start my tribute to Margie with this: I sent an Angel to watch over you, and she came back laughing. When I asked why she was laughing, she said, "You don't need to have an Angel watch over another Angel!" And that is exactly how I always saw Margie. She was there for me countless times, whether over the phone or in person. She always made me feel loved and safe. She would fight and protect the underdog, even at the risk of what others would say. She nursed the Spirit, the body, and the Soul, never asking for anything in return. When my own world turned upside down, she righted it enough for me to be able to limp along.

We spent hours and hours together, always talking about whatever we felt was important and sometimes about absolutely nothing. We went on retreats together where we shared our beliefs and wonder in all that is creation. She loved openly, stubbornly, and without complication. We shared sorrows and joys. Her family was her pride, and she had an extended family of an assortment of people whom she took under her wings. She gave whatever she could, often at her own peril, and rejoiced when it did good for the recipient. To this day I have never met anyone who believed in a God as innocently as did she, except for my own mother. That belief I was lucky enough to share with Margie, and I knew if anyone had a little place waiting in Heaven, it had to be her. Till we meet again, my Friend, my Sister, and God's own Angel!

Chapter 10

Margie's Message

The Legacy

My Mother believed that there is such a thing as extraterrestrial life. "For us to think we are the only ones in this vast universe is narrow-minded. How can that be possible here amongst all the millions of stars?" she would say.

Helping Beyond Life

My sister Julie had shared with me that towards the end of Mom's life, one of the nurses looking after Mom at the hospital had pulled her aside and said, "I've worked in this business for many years and your mother's failing is beyond physical, it's emotional."

Mom was slipping away, becoming more withdrawn. Ultimately, dementia would take the rest of her from us. She was not able to continue to impart her heart to me and others.

Although I do not pretend to have any psychic powers, my gut instinct and my Mom's teachings to listen to the inner voice, helped me know that she would be looking out for us after she passed on. I believe that towards the end of her life, she realized she was trapped in a worn-out body, and if she released herself into death, as a spirit, she could access all she needed to assist and help others.

I strongly believe that my sister and I came up with the idea for this book because Mom guided us to it. She inspired me to write these stories to experience her love and her way with others in a more profound way, to impact all who knew her with the stories I shared in this book and continue seeking and discovering joy and a better life for ourselves and our loved ones.

Is that not what everyone wants?

Butterflies and Sunsets

During the writing of this book, I was visited again by a butterfly. There I sat in bumper-to-bumper traffic on Highway, 401, making my way out of Toronto to my home. I rolled all four windows down to change the air in my truck. It was a cool fall afternoon. The song by Whitney Houston, "I Love the Lord" came on the radio. I referenced this song earlier in this book and how it played while my mother and I drove through Forks of the Credit area by my home. As I reached to turn up the volume, a white butterfly entered in through the passenger window and flew right in front of me, then exited my driver window. I strained my neck to watch it by sticking my head out my truck window. The butterfly flew straight up and out of my sight.

When I see butterflies, it reminds me that Mom is always with me.

One evening as I was driving home from a meeting and the sun was setting in front of me, Mom came into my mind. Just as I had this very intense thought about her, the setting sun turned the entire sky pink in an instant.

Mom's favourite colour was pink.

I interpreted this as her saying, "Good night, and I'm here to remind you that every time you see a pink sunset, I'm with you."

I realized as I experienced this, that people do not leave us. They leave a part of them in us always, and as we honour ourself after they have passed on, we honour them as well.

Recently a friend visited me, and we spent the better part of a day together. He expressed to me how he had contemplated suicide the night before. He had come really close, and my mother had brought him to me, sending him to come and see me at my home.

I am very happy to report that my friend is doing well now. And despite having never been interested in anything psychically related, this friend even went to a psychic who told him, "Margie is there for you, and when you smell flowers, it is her."

Margie's Messages

Margie's calming nature

Mom cooed at, spoke, sang, and hummed to babies and animals, instantly calming them, bonding souls with them. We often heard her humming all over our home while she did the daily chores.

Mom used to say, "Get quiet and trust your inner voice. Your inner voice will guide you." Mom believed that we all have the ability to know what to do in any situation or in any decision we have to make.

Margie's definition of integrity

Do the right thing always, especially when no one is watching. You will always know what the right thing to do is by checking in and listening to your inner voice.

"Love you"

She showed she cared with both words and deeds.

Mom once talked to a lady in a lineup in a bank's lobby for ten minutes. The bank manager came to get Mom for their meeting, and leaving the waiting room, Mom said to the woman, "Nice speaking with you, dear. Love you." By the way the lady reacted, it seemed as if she had not had anyone say, "Love you" to her for a very, very long time.

Mom believed we are all connected, especially with those in our lives

Mom used to say if you haven't heard from someone in your life for a while and you think about them or they come into your mind two or three times, pick up the phone and call them.

Difficult times

If you were having a hard time and you shared it with her, she would say, "Put the light of God around you." If it was a very difficult time for you, she would add, "And I will do the same."

How can I better understand this person I have an issue with?

If Mom had a problem with someone, she would say, "I need to sit down and have a listen with them." She worded it this way because she saw this opportunity to better understand that person.

I have often wondered what this world would look like if others followed this approach, if people asked themselves the above question, instead of giving someone a piece of their mind or sorting them out.

Mom believed that we are spiritual beings having a human experience.

This is why life can be such a challenge for us. We have never dealt with emotional pain, fear, frustration, anger, resentment, anxiety, and the biggest one—betrayal. So we are not any good at it. She would say, "When these emotions and feelings come up for you, be patient with yourself. You don't know how to do any of this. But know this for sure: you will always be okay."

G.O.D. is Good, Orderly Direction

If someone was uncomfortable with the term God, Mom would say, "Okay, how about this? G.O.D. stands for Good, Orderly Direction. Everybody wants that, yes?"

Mom believed that all religions are equal

Mom also believed that through their own religion, people are searching for spiritual meaning, which she defined as "The Higher Power" or "The Source."

Mom believed we are all children of God

She believed we are the hands and fingers of God. But we have to make a conscious decision to use them.

Mom always said...

"There's far too much emphasis on Jesus. He was the *messenger*. The emphasis should be on his *message*. When religion expresses to you to give your life to Jesus, I believe it's the Jesus in each of us we should give ourselves to, instead of the separate Jesus who lived."

She believed there have been many messengers and they continue to come into this world. Buddha is another example of a messenger.

Helping awaken the need to help one another

Mom loved the television show, *Touched by an Angel*. She said, "I am so happy to see this type of topic being covered by the television industry. We need more of these types of stories. They help wake people up to how we need to be there for one another."

She believed in a higher power that is always there, especially in our darkest times.

Oprah Winfrey, Mom's hero

Mom was a faithful follower of Oprah and *The Oprah Winfrey Show*. Sometimes she called family members or friends to tell them about that day's guest on the show, describing in detail how the interview touched her.

She loved what Oprah represented. "If a poor, African-American female and rape victim can rise to such greatness, it is possible for everyone to aim and work for happiness and success."

Mom marvelled at Oprah's ability to be such a conduit that represented love and caring through her show, inspiring and paying forward wherever and whenever she could.

What Mom Taught Me

Take responsibility for how others respond to me in everything I say or do with them.

Do the right thing always, especially when no one is watching. Always think of the needs of others.

If I am upset about something in my life, take the focus off myself and go and help someone else.

Do my best. Try my best. Do not give up.

Listen more than I speak, especially during a conflict.

Forgive.

Let go of my busy mind so I can be with someone and see them, hear them, and be truly present.

I am the hands and fingers of God, and I must use them.

To love another is actually a gift I give myself.

Margie's Sayings

Luverly - Lovely and very special.

Go on with you - Margie did not agree with you.

Slop-jock - If my shirt was not tucked in or my room was untidy.

Trust your inner voice - You have the answers you are looking for inside yourself.

Heavens to Betsy - When she was pleasantly surprised.

Put the light of God around you - If you had a problem in your life.

Put the light of God around you and I will do the same - If you had a big problem.

Change the station - Change what you're thinking about to a positive thought.

Never you mind - It is not your concern.

Godincidence - It is not a coincidence, for God is behind everything.

Thank you for being in my life - A common statement she wrote in greeting cards.

I'm *thrilled* for you - When you shared great news from your life with her. You could feel her excitement and admiration as she said the word thrilled.

I'm going to fix'm - When she took on a new person in her life she would be helping, or referring to a new dog that we brought into our home who may not have, been treated properly in the past.

Mom's Final Message

Despite it being difficult for her to write because of Parkinson's, Mom sent this passage to Jules her final Christmas with us. It encapsulates what she imparted to all of us. It was something Margie read in a book called *The Messengers* years ago. She cited it to me in conversation many times. I connected with one of the book's co-authors, Julia Ingram, to ask for permission to include the passage in this book. Here it is:

> *You must believe in yourself at all times. You must never lose faith that you are capable of doing anything in life you choose to do. And you must always choose the highest. It is not enough for you to choose that you must achieve excellence. For you must believe in yourself enough to accomplish that which others cannot accomplish. To believe in yourself, you must have courage that exceeds the need for the conversation of courage. It must be a natural part of your life that voids any decision-making based on whether you have the courage to do what must be done. This must be a*

belief beyond personal questioning, beyond personal doubt, to a point when it can no longer be considered courage, but rather a way of life. This shall be so, for you will believe in yourself.

You must have character that is beyond criticism and is a permanent part of yourself. It is not imagined or pretended. Every moment of your life must be naturally conducted with pride and dignity that cannot be confused with arrogance, but recognized with respect. Your character must always contain compassion and concern for others.

This concern will be genuine, for you will never lose sight of your background in trying to understand those you have difficulty identifying with, for they are the majority of the world and the ones who need it the most.

You must believe in yourself so that your character is consistent, never bends and never compromises.

You must believe in your intellect that no task is beyond your ability to succeed. Your intellect is a gift that you shall not waste and you shall use to its greatest capacity.

You must have the patience and tolerance to realize others will not always agree with or understand you. But rather than find fault, you shall try harder to reach them, for it shall become your responsibility to serve them.

This is your calling. You cannot question it. You must accept it.

Let this be your daily manifesto, with the intention to create an infrastructure for a better world.

Merry Christmas!

Epilogue

From Me to You

In the preface of this book, I wrote about my flight to Cayo Coco in Cuba on my way to making some important decisions. I now close by sharing with you what happened upon my arrival home from that trip.

As the taxi pulled into my driveway at 1:30 am on that Sunday night, I saw my brother-in-law standing on my back porch. My nineteen-year-old nephew was in jail. This boy had been in and out of trouble since he was twelve.

Gavin's parents were at the end of their rope. I immediately agreed to help.

I stood in front of a judge the following morning and was awarded my nephew's release. That afternoon, when we entered the house together, I explained to Gavin that the standard operating procedure at our home was to get up before 9 am and make our beds.

He asked about other rules and I said we would add them as we rolled. I also expressed that as much as my son Reigan and I were here to help him, he was here to help us.

He asked, "How do I help you?" "You'll figure that out," I said.

He did figure it out. He cleaned, helped me with computer issues, and even formulated a door-to-door campaign to promote my lighting business.

During the first week he lived with us, he planned how he would commit to and succeed in his recovery. His parents had provided him with quite a list. He agreed to almost everything and added a few of his own actions. To that list he added writing a daily journal, writing music, and producing rap recordings.

During this first week, something also occurred that saddened me deeply. Warren, the boy I referred to earlier in this book, had lost his battle with life.

I got the phone call while driving with my nephew. Warren's sister let me know her brother had been pronounced dead at 8:02 pm the previous night.

I had to pull my truck over to collect myself.

Gavin witnessed my reaction to this phone call. I then immediately phoned my youngest sister who had worked with me to help Warren. Gavin and I sat in silence and the phone remained on speaker. When I told Julie that Warren was gone, she screamed, "No!" three times and fell apart.

It took her a few moments to regulate her breathing and calm down. Then she said, "I'll be okay. Let me call you later."

After she hung up, Gavin and I remained silent. Then I said, "That's the phone call."

He looked at me, and I stared directly into his eyes and explained, "The call your parents and all of us have been afraid we'd receive about *you*."

Sometimes life can hit you in the head.

I think for Gavin, this was one of those times.

I often think about that call and wonder about how and why things happen the way they do—how, out of tragedy, a lesson can be received. Was this an indirect way for Warren to have a chance to help Gavin in his recovery? Perhaps my mother—Gavin's grandmother—was helping him through me, to help Gavin realize where he was headed.

Gavin received his one-year AA medallion, and it was wonderful to be there to support him in this milestone along with his parents and brother.

That night, I looked at my nephew sitting in the front seat, and many thoughts went through my head. I was happy to be part of his recovery over the time he lived with us. I was so proud of him, and I was also proud of my son for his contributions to his cousin.

I believe all people have an inherent desire to help others.

During the September 11 World Trade Center tragedy, the way the New York community came together to help each other further highlighted that desire in us to help others in "our hour of need."

The way many people all over the world reach out and help others gives me hope for a brighter tomorrow.

As my mother taught me, there is no better feeling than that sense of joy and fulfillment when you can help another soul along their life journey.

May I leave you with this final thought? I read this in the *New York Times*. It references a book being written about Pope Francis by Austen Ivereigh: "It is better to live a shorter life serving others than a longer one resisting that call."

My hope is that this book has not only introduced you to Margie but also given you a relationship with her. As you go forward in your life, perhaps these stories will come to mind. If that happens, know that it is possible that it is Margie checking in with you, letting you know that she is there for you, letting you know that it is always going to be all right.

She may even come to you in the fragrance of a flower or as you notice a white butterfly in flight.

God Bless,

Tom

"Read it Forward" Initiative:

At the beginning of this book you perused a 2nd Line West title page with my signature. At the top of the page is the following:

To: _____

To: _____

To: _____

My intention for writing this book was always the opportunity for me to share my mothers approach to living life with others. As you have read this book and now that you have completed your read, if someone in your life has come to mind who might enjoy this read, my hope is that you consider sharing it with them.

Simply add their name to the line after "To:" and hand it to them or mail it to them.

I believe people read books for 3 reasons:

to escape

to exercise their imagination

to learn

But I also believe that a book can change someone's life.

If you decide to keep the book for yourself that is just fine as well.

God Bless,
TH

Acknowledgments

Jules: For never giving up on me and saving me from myself many times over. You coached me to keep going on this project, especially when I wondered if I could ever pull this off. I love you forever, JJ.

Tanya Freedman: Editor and publisher of the first edition of this book. Thank you for your gentle guidance and your caring hand, which has led me on this path. As I stated when we sat beside each other on the plane for the second time in one week, our paths crossing was a "Godincidence" and not merely a coincidence.

My sister, Julie: Thank you for helping with this book's story content, consultation, and moral support. You generously arranged, conducted, and transcribed the interviews for this project. We began as a team and came out of this collaboration with a spiritual connection over and above a brother and sister bond. Thanks "Mowsters."

My sister, Valerie: Thank you for helping confirm details from the past. Before Google, there was Valerie.

Lee Cole: Thank you for sharing the letters Mom had written to you. I look forward to our next dinner together.

My son, Reigan: For being all that I could have ever asked for and more. I am proud of you.

My nephew, Gavin: For being an example of how it is possible to change your life once you decide.

My sister, Cynthia: For all of our wonderful shared memories of our past.

Danny Hall and Tommy Hall, David Moore and Dylan Moore.

Elaine Weise: Thank you for giving us that visual of Mom when you first met. It was perfect!

Bonnie Kogos: Thank you for your counsel on this project. You are a breath of fresh air, Auntie Bubbles!

Austin and Natalia for your invaluable feedback on this book.

Frank, Gloria, and Cathy: For all your love and support with this project.

Steve Micros: For providing me with the picture of Reigan and me. You are a great photographer, my friend.

Richard Hanlon, our brother from another ... wait ... no, from the same mother.

Colin Forrester: Take the time to smell the flowers, my friend.

Darlene Morris: Our family appreciates your special friendship. You are also an example of how truth liberates us. God Bless and RIP.

Steven Harrison: You helped me understand my true potential and how to pursue it in the right way. Your company helps people plant their dream seeds and holds their hand to harvest.

Father Gregory Boyle for blessing this book with these words:

"May you continue to be a remarkable sign of the God who loves us without measure and without regret. May your Mom's spirit live on in all this."

Laura Palletta: You are another soul who helped me know I was onto something worth completing. Stay the course, my friend. The world needs more like you. Thank you for your letter.

Tristan Emanuel: Thank you for helping me understand I had an idea worth exploring, and for all your efforts to start this project on its path.

Warren Dankovic: You are with your Auntie again for sure, and we miss you.

All AA members: You gave us our mother back. Your universal commitment to families represents the message in this book. Well done, Bill W!

Nana: For your strength and teaching us that love is expressed in deeds and not with our mouths.

Gramps: Who I am named after, thanks for teaching us how to honour ourselves with truth.

Grandpa: My maternal grandfather, who gave me my middle name, Daniel. Thank you for helping support Mom in so many ways.

Grandma: You represent forgiveness.

To all the other friends who contributed to our project and our lives with their presence in these stories: Iris, Laurie, Diane, Dr. Trimble, Don Canning, Auntie Helen, Bob Campbell, David Campbell, Dr. Leroy Franklin, Lou, Auntie Ann, Auntie Cathy, Barbie, Bernice, and Craig.

Jim Carrey: "The effect you have on others is the most valuable currency there is." When I heard you say this at MUM Commencement in 2014, I knew I had to finish this book. Thank you for that invaluable inspiration.

Oprah Winfrey: Margie Herstad lived your commitment to creating a better world. A world with more love.

Marianne Williamson: Our mother followed your lead in *A Course in Miracles*.

Rosie: Thank you for your story. Please contact us. We would love to connect with you again.

Paul Morin: Thank you for helping me on my journey. Until such time.

Harvey: Thank you for finding the pictures we needed. Writing this book has reconnected me with many great friends, and you are another wonderful example of this.

Lisa Cauda at Rochester Institute of Technology: I submitted the first publication of this book to you and you accepted it as my first year English course, never completed, giving me a credit by experience. As a result, in 2017, I drove to Rochester to receive my Bachelor of Science in Marketing. So thirty years after I left RIT in 1987 I did in fact receive my degree. "It's never too late, to finish something you have begun" Tom Herstad

Mary Hill: For your valuable feedback early in this project. I will always remember your dinner prayer.

Edmundo: For your commitment to helping me evolve.

Maureen Jenkins: For your heartfelt letter included in this book.

Dawn: For your beautiful letter included in this book.

Sean The Bomb, Dana, Darcy, Kim and Matt Scanlon, Teddy, Henrietta, blue jays, and butterflies.

David Labadie: Thank you for your contribution to this book with your heartfelt letter. RIP my friend.

Carolyn VanBrussel: Thank you for seeing a grander meaning in my endeavour and

helping me understand my work is surely "Where Light Meets Life."

Joel Osteen: You represent the power of positivity and possibility.

My Dad, Gerald Thomas Herstad: For showing me charisma, love, and a zest for life that still remains in the memories of all who knew you.

My Mom, Mary Margaret Herstad: For being the most extraordinary example of how we can experience love, if we allow ourselves. You have always been my true example. Until we meet again, I will honour your presence in my life every day. You are truly a "Messenger" whose message is celebrated. Sugar Fella Boo loves you!

The Backstory

While engaging in discussions about our mother's life in 2011, shortly after her memorial service, I stated, "Mom's story should be a book and perhaps even a movie." Little did I know at the time the many things that would happen during this story-writing process—including a movie contract being confirmed with Sunrise Films.

If you're interested in the details of how this book, its writing, and the movie contract happened, I share all the steps involved and all the serendipitous events that occurred all along this magical path in the blog section of the book's website: www.tomherstadofficial.com

If you visit the website, feel free to leave a comment or a short review of the book. I enjoy very much hearing from readers and their thoughts on this story.

About the Author

Over the last twenty-five years, Tom Herstad has had a profound impact on the people he has dealt with in a variety of industries. He has led and inspired people within Fortune 500 companies. As an avid coach of young hockey talent, Tom has also encouraged family and friends to empower themselves, all the while continuing his mother's legacy, to help others to achieve their own full potential and find joy in the everyday.

Since 2002, Tom has built a busy, successful LED lighting business, based in Toronto, Canada, shedding physical light on people's lives. Inspired by Jim Carrey's message that the effect you have on others is the most valuable currency there is, Tom was drawn to complete his five-year spiritual journey, culminating in this book. Taking a sabbatical away from his busy schedule, he set out to share his mother's life story, her message, and what he learned. Through this book, Tom's achievements in making light meet life are complemented with spiritual development. And he is grateful to you, the reader.